becoming
GOOD
parents

4 F's

AFFECTION
FAIRNESS
FLEXIBILITY
FIRMNESS

SUNY Series, Alternatives in Psychology
Michael A. Wallach, editor

becoming
GOOD
parents

an existential journey

Mufid James Hannush

State University of New York Press

Published by
State University of New York Press, Albany

© 2002 State University of New York

For information, address State University of New York Press,
90 State Street, Suite 700, Albany, NY 12207

Production by Dana Foote
Marketing by Michael Campochiaro

Library of Congress Cataloging-in-Publication Data

Hannush, Mufid James, 1945–
    Becoming good parents : an existential journey / Mufid James Hannush.
        p. cm. — (SUNY series, alternatives in psychology)
    Includes bibliographical references and index.
    ISBN 0-7914-5461-4 (alk. paper) — ISBN 0-7914-5462-2 (pbk. : alk. paper)
        1. Parenting—Psychological aspects. 2. Parents—Attitudes. 3. Parent and child.
    I. Title. II. Series

HQ755.8 .H334 2002
649'.1—dc21   2002066958

10 9 8 7 6 5 4 3 2 1

This book, which is a labor of love and gratitude, is dedicated to my bright, brave, and beautiful daughter, Vera, who continues to teach me how to become a good parent.

Contents

Acknowledgments

To acknowledge is to, at least in part, be grateful and/or affirm the mattering of essential others to my life's journey in general or the completion of the present book in particular.

To, and in memory of, my mother and father, Atiya and James; my aunts and uncles, Janet and Ibrahim, Louisa and Ishak, and Rosa and Hilmy; my grandparents, Anna and Abdul Messiah and Zarifa and Said, who demonstrated through their exemplary lives the human capacities for forgiveness and for rising above the tragedies that befell their families as a consequence of the genocide and the uprooting of the Armenians, Assyrians, and other Christian minorities in Turkey.

To my sister, Deniz, who encouraged me to translate my ideas into book form. To my brothers and their wives: Maria and Wasim and Darlene and Robert. To my brother Muzid. To my uncles and aunts, Joseph and Joan and Basim and Lameece. To all my cousins, especially Samir, Suheil, Sadeer, Neçip, Ann, and Joey, and to my nieces and nephews.

To Lois Hannush, Emma Null, Mary and George Null, Vicki Mrak, and Jan Racca.

To my friends Munther Jabbur, Amin Kassis, and Suheil Khuri, who unceasingly urged me to move on to the next chapter. To: Richard Buchkam, Steven and Barbara Morrow, C. Patrick Williams, and all those who remain unnamed.

To Rosemont College for granting me the sabbatical that launched the present project. To Margie Crawford, who extended her secretarial assistance above and beyond the call of duty. To my colleagues, Tom Carney (in memoriam), Amedeo Giorgi, and Jackie Murphy, for graciously proofreading the copyedited manuscript.

To Jane Bunker, senior editor at SUNY Press, who resonated to the book project while it was incomplete and supported its completion. To Dana Foote, production editor, whose delightful diligence in managing the production of the book was deeply appreciated. To Kay Bolton, for her methodical manner in copyediting the manuscript. To Michael Campochiaro, Marketing Manager, for his expertise.

To the two reviewers of my work, Scott Churchill and Frank C. Richardson, whose high praise was deeply gratifying and whose excellent suggestions added to the further refinement of the book.

To all my undergraduate and graduate students who have inspired me throughout my twenty years of teaching.

Introduction

It is never too late to be what you might have been.✳
—George Eliot

What does it mean to be good and loving parents?[1] This book aims at fleshing out the meaning of good and loving parenting. Its goal is to describe the essential elements that make up the structure of good and loving parenting. Although it offers no "how to" techniques and strategies for the achievement of good parenting, it holds the conviction that an in-depth description of the theoretical structure of good and loving parenting leads to an understanding that can inspire change in our consciousness and actions. "The chief value of a parental theory," writes Jane Loevinger (1959), "may well be in providing a model for the child of curbing one's own impulses out of regard for the future welfare of another" (p. 150). What Loevinger does not say, but implicitly implies, is that parenting, therefore, is ultimately an existential and ethical human endeavor. A good parental theory offers a prescription for living (existing) morally, not only for the sake of the children *and* their parents, but also out of care and concern for the welfare of future generations.

The intention of this book is to live up to Loevinger's envisioned value of a parental theory. Unlike, yet in some ways complementary to, many books and textbooks on parenting (e.g., Brooks, 2001; Faber and Mazlish, 1980; Gordon, 1975; Hammer and Turner, 1996; Lickona, 1983; Martin and Colbert, 1997), this text adopts a metapsychological prespective.[2] That is, it goes beyond providing simply a psychological understanding of parenting. It attempts to present a parental theory that is grounded in an existential understanding of the human person.[3] Its approach, as the existential psychologist Rollo May would put it, is "psycho-ontological." The term "ontology" is derived from the Greek "ontos" (being) and "logos" (knowledge or meaning). The answer to the question What does it mean to be good and loving parents? lies in answering the larger question What does it mean to be good and loving persons or human beings? Paradoxically, the reverse is also true. In other words, we learn to become good and loving human beings by becoming good and loving parents, and we become better parents as we become better persons. This existential paradox applies to other vocations or roles as well—for example, being a teacher, a son, a sister, or a friend.

1

Parenting, in this book, is viewed as an existential life project that has far-reaching implications for the psychosocial and moral growth of both children *and* parents. The presupposition is made that love is indispensable for the attainment of human goodness. The analogous presumption is that the capacity to love is essential for moral development and personality integration.

One overriding assumption in this book is that parenting needs to be "good" and not simply "good enough;" that parenting, as an ethical life project, requires constant moral vigilance; that parenting, as a spiritual endeavor, necessitates a perpetual inspiration by the idea of goodness. Some psychologists and writers of developmental psychology textbooks, such as Sandra Scarr (1992) and Judith Rich Harris (1998), contend that because children's development and growth is primarily dictated by nature (genetic influences), parenting patterns are not important. Parents, therefore, need to be merely "good enough."4 Scarr (1992) states:

> Children's outcomes do not depend on whether parents take (them) to a ball game or a museum so much as they depend on genetic transmission, on plentiful opportunities, and having a *good enough* environment that supports children's development to become themselves. (p.15; emphasis added)

Taking children to museums, and thus exposing them to the idea of the beautiful (and the good), can contribute to the cultivation and refinement of their character. Diana Baumrind (1993) criticizes Scarr's stance on parenting. She points out that there are wide variations in what constitutes "good enough" parenting which are likely to have a great impact on children's developmental outcomes. Baumrind is concerned that advising parents to simply be "good enough" may incline them to be less committed in fostering their children's growth and to feel less responsible should their children fail.

Harris (1998) draws the attention of parents in the following manner: "Parenting has been oversold. You have been led to believe that you have more influence over your child's personality than you really do" (p. 351). Like Scarr, Harris does not totally rule out parental influence on children, especially in circumstances which fall far outside of the normal range, such as when parents are abusive or neglectful. Although similar to Scarr in her emphasis on the critical influence of genetic factors, Harris points out the importance of peers, not parents, in shaping and modifying children's behavior as they develop into adulthood. For Harris, then, genetic makeup and peer relations are the primary shapers of children's development and growth. Bandura (1986) counters the peer influence argument very convincingly. He says that when children and adolescents gravitate toward adopting the self-evaluative standards of their peers rather than their parents or other adults in their lives, it is because they can more easily live up to the lower standards set by their peers. Parents and other significant adult figures, according to Bandura, can engage in actions or make use of strategies to get children to adopt higher self-evaluative standards. For instance, parents can encourage their children to associate with peers who are high achieving and have high self-evaluative standards. Parents themselves, who have established a strong and positive affectional tie with their children, can serve as high-achieving models with high self-evaluative standards. Parents can also expose their children to models who are either externally rewarded or internally self-reinforced for living up to high standards. Parents can read to their children stories about famous historical or contemporary figures who pursued excellence and eventually gained recognition. Children naturally imitate and identify with parents who consistently care for and love them. They internalize their parents' standards of excellence and make them their own.

According to Heinz Kohut (1971, 1977, 1978, 1984), children are naturally driven by ambitions for power, success, and healthy expansiveness. They are at the same time pulled by ideals and idealized goals and values. In other words, they need their parents and essential others as targets of idealization. Moreover, they need to recognize themselves in similar others. They not only want to be loved, empathically understood, and validated ("mirrored") by their parents, they also want to increase their similarity to them by imitating, identifying (merging) with, and internalizing the values and ideals of these essential others. Under relatively optimal familial and societal conditions, which allow for self-care promoting parental failures and frustrations, children grow toward becoming their true selves. In brief (for a detailed discussion of these ideas see chapter 2), propelled by a natural need for expansiveness ("grandiosity"), children are simultaneously pulled by their complementary need to increase their similarity to idealizable others. Becoming good parents, therefore, means becoming worthy of idealization. It means serving as competent, efficacious, and "moral exemplars" (Damon, 1988).

Attachment theorists John Bowlby and Mary Ainsworth (Ainsworth and Bowlby, 1991) and their followers (see Cassidy and Shaver, 1999; Karen, 1998) have garnered impressive evidence suggesting that it is parental responsiveness and not innate temperament that is the critical factor in the nature (genetics)-versus-nurture (parental influence) debate. Jerome Kagan (1984) argues that attachment theorists and researchers ignore the role of innate temperament. According to Kagan, some infants are innately fearless; others are innately fearful or shy and withdrawn. Although Kagan does not ignore the influence of parents and the social environment, he takes the position that these influences are limited in the face of enduring genetically based traits. Bowlby (1982) distills the position of attachment theory in this manner:[5]

> An easy newborn may assist an uncertain mother to develop a favorable pattern of care. Conversely, a difficult unpredictable newborn may tip the balance the other way. Yet all the evidence shows that a potentially easy baby is still likely to develop unfavorably if given unfavorable care and also, more

fortunately, that with only few exceptions a potentially difficult baby can develop favorably if given sensitive care. The capacity of a sensitive mother to adapt to even a difficult unpredictable baby and thereby enable him to develop favorably is perhaps the most heartening of all recent findings in this field. (p. 368)

Kagan hopes that research on temperament will take the pressure off parents. Here is Kagan quoted in Karen (1998):

There are some people with a very short fuse. They blow up easily; it's hard to get along with them. Many people assume that it's a function of their past and they should be able to control it. So then you get angry at these people. But if you believe that this is partly temperamental, and their biology prepares them for this, then you become a little more forgiving. (p. 296)

There are parents in this world who have "very short fuses" and who "blow up easily" at their children. These parents may have very young children who are, by temperament, either resilient and easily forgiving or fragile, difficult, and not so easily forgiving. Hearing Kagan's message, these parents may come to view themselves as "good enough" parents in spite of the differential, deleterious, and cumulative impact of their uncontrolled outbursts upon their children. Some children may fare better than others under these familial circumstances. However, this does not absolve parents of the responsibility for their abusive verbal or nonverbal behavior. Parents who, by temperament, are prone to outbursts of anger and rage can learn to become calm and collected. Parenting itself provides the opportunity for such learning to occur. This is not an easy task. It requires hard work. The process of parenting involves not only teaching children to become responsible citizens and good persons, it also allows parents to learn to become better human beings themselves. Becoming good parents is becoming good persons. "Finding oneself dealing well with the emotional challenges of parenthood can . . . be a transforming experience" (Karen, 1998, p. 405). Parenting provides us with repeated opportunities to confront ourselves and discover who we are and the kind of persons we want to become. "The problem we have as parents, then, is not usually a lack of love or good intentions, but more often an unwillingness to *face who we are.* Obviously, this failure has other implications for adult psychology, as well" (Karen 1998, p. 378; emphasis added).

This brings us to the second assumption of this text: Good parenting can foster not only the growth of children, but also the intellectual, emotional, moral, and spiritual growth of parents. Additionally, it can make their lives existentially significant or meaningful. According to Newman and Newman (1999), "Parenting may bring new levels of insight, intellectual flexibility, and social commitment" (p. 448). "Parenting contributes to the expansion of caring" (p. 449).

Through caring for their children and meeting their needs, parents deepen their level of commitment. By playing a significant role in the lives of their children, parents experience an enhancement in their own value and well-being. Parenting provides parents with new channels for the expression of a wide variety of emotions. It allows them to deepen their capacity for love and empathy. By helping their children to express and understand emotions, parents can learn to comprehend and modulate their own emotions. Through parenting, parents are forced to examine their own goals and values and thus are enabled to formulate a philosophy of life. Through becoming attuned to the differential strengths and limitations of their children, parents are afforded the opportunity to learn to be accepting, affirming, and respectful of these differences, including differences in temperaments. The process of parenting, say Newman and Newman, gives parents the chance to "review their own development . . . [and] realize how far they have come in their own efforts at self-definition" (1999, p. 448). Through parenting, parents can experience an expansion in their consciousness. Parenting potentially brings with it "a new perspective on time, purpose, and meaning of life" (Newman and Newman, 1999, p. 448). Parents can grow through learning how to constructively resolve conflicts with their children.

> Parenting is stressful. It is full of conflicts and challenges . . . however . . . parenting generates the kind of conflict that promises an enormous potential for personal growth. . . . Psychological growth requires a willingness to engage in tasks that may temporarily increase stress, uncertainty and complexity. Thus, it does not mean turning away from or minimizing tension. It frequently means choosing the challenge that is noticeably difficult or intriguingly complex in hopes of growing while struggling to meet it. (Newman and Newman, 1999, p. 449)

More than fifty years ago, Arthur Jersild and his colleagues interviewed parents about the "joys and problems" of raising children. Here is what they had to say about parenthood: "Perhaps no other circumstance in life offers so many challenges to an individual's powers, so great an array of opportunities for appreciation, such as varied emotional and intellectual stimulations" (quoted in Brooks, 2001, p. 100). That was in 1948. In 1975, David Guttman interviewed parents about the impact of having children on their lives. His conclusion was: "For most adult humans, parenthood is still the ultimate source of the sense of meaning. For most adults the question What does life mean? is automatically answered once they have children; better yet it is no longer asked" (quoted in Brooks, 2001, p. xvii). In 1991, when parents were asked about the advantages and disadvantages of parenthood by Carolyn and Philip Cowan, two advantages were mentioned that are worth singling out: "Experiencing new growth and learning opportunities that add meaning to life" and "Learning to become less selfish and to sacrifice" (quoted in Berk, 2001, p. 472). And in *Between Generations: The Six Stages of Parenthood*, Ellen Galinsky (1981) gives a summary of how the parenting process changes parents:

> Taking care of a small, dependent, growing person is transforming, because it brings us in touch with our baser side, it exposes our vulnerabilities as well as our nobility. We lose our sense of self, only to find it change again and again. We learn to nurture and care. We struggle through defining our own rules and our own brand of being an authority. We figure out how we want to interpret the wider world, and we learn to interact with all those who affect our children. When our children are teenagers, we redefine our relationships, and then we launch them into life.
>
> Often our fantasies are laid bare, our dreams are in a constant tug of war with realities. And perhaps we grow. In the end, we have learned more about ourselves, about the cycles of life, and humanity itself. Most parents describe themselves as more responsible, more accepting, more generous than before they had children. (p. 317)

The parenting experience, therefore, bestows upon us multiple opportunities to confront our own "vulnerabilities," control our "baser side," and achieve "nobility" of character. Through the parenting experience, we learn not only about "ourselves," but also about belonging to the continuing "cycles of life" and a universal "humanity" of which we are a part. Through parenting, we learn to become more "accepting," "generous," and "responsible." Additionally, we learn to become more empathic, loving, patient, and self-sacrificing. Simply stated, we become more ourselves as we approach the essential meaning of our humanity. The ending of the second assumption flows into the third interrelated assumption of this book: Along with other modalities of existence parenting is an existential journey which makes possible the refining of our human character. Through parenting, we learn about who we are and who we can become as human beings. True, parenting can bring out the worst in us. But, it can also bring out the best in us. Parenting has the potential of heightening our reflective awareness. Our children mirror us back to ourselves. I remember listening to an interview with a former member of a fascist hate- and violence-prone group. In this interview on national public radio, he was asked what made him quit the group and join an organization whose mission was to reduce the likelihood of other young and vulnerable youth joining such potentially destructive organizations. His answer was that the pivotal transformation occurred when he heard his very young child mirroring hate phrases targeted toward members of other ethnic and racial groups. He came to the realization that he did not want his child to become the kind of person he had become. This was his moment of truth and transformation.

Children are not the only ones who grow as a consequence of good parenting, says Brooks (2001). Through effective parenting, parents themselves grow physically, in terms of agility and stamina, intellectually, through being constantly cognitively challenged and made vigilant by the presence of their children, and emotionally, through experiencing intense feelings, both positive and negative, learning to modulate and regulate these feelings as well as those of their children, while attempting to make their feelings in addition to the feelings of their children understandable. "In helping new life grow, we gain for ourselves an inner vitality and richness that affects all our relationships" (Brooks, 2001, p. xix). According to Galatzer-Levy and Cohler (1993), viewing themselves as good or competent parents is vitally important to their sense of well-being. Just as parents are important significant others for their children, children "are essential others for their parents, providing support for the parents' experience of a cohesive self and innumerable opportunities for the development of the parents' self. A major support for the experience of self in adult life is the sense of filling defined social roles" (Galatzer-Levy and Cohler, pp. 227–28). But above all, "[p]arents have the privilege of serving as guide and resource as their child creates a unique psychological self" (Brooks, 2001, p. 124).

Our children repeatedly inspire and invite us to become our better selves. This is why parenting can be viewed as a vocation, a calling: the calling of our innermost conscience to become ourselves, to become our essential (true) character. Becoming good parents requires of us keeping intact and inviolate, as much as humanly possible, our innermost character. Our children need to idealize us. We, as parents, are called to be worthy of such idealization. We can either succeed or fail at refining our character. Of course, there are degrees of success and failure. Becoming a good person/parent is never easy. In *The Risk of Being: What It Means to Be Good and Bad*, the existential philosopher Michael Gelven (1997) states that to succeed as characters we must reflect upon or mirror who we are. As mentioned earlier, our children constantly mirror who we are. We need to vigilantly step back and take stock of who we are becoming in the light of such mirroring.

In a previous part of the introduction, an opposition was created between genetic influences and parental (an other environmental) influences.[6] No leeway was left for at least a limited sense of agency (freedom). Gelven (1997) constructs a division between genetic and parental (environmental) influences on the one hand and the role we play in the making of our individual character on the other hand. For Gelven (1997),

> character seems [to be] the fundamental seat of judgment, strength, responsibility, and guilt. It is the one term we seem to identify most closely with our reality. My character is my Self and, for whatever reason, this character identifies me with who I am. Character seems the personification of the "principle of individuation." (p.35)

To be human, for Gelven, always involves being constantly at risk of becoming a good (noble) or bad (ignoble) character. Being human, according to Gelven

(2000), also involves being perpetually suspended between the essential polarities of our existence. "Suspension seems to be of our essence . . . : we neither know everything nor do we lack knowledge entirely; our existence is neither necessary nor impossible. It is as possible that we hang suspended between everything and nothing, God and beast, the absolute and the nugatory" (Gelven, 2000, p. 15). However, between the extremes of the necessary (the limits set by our genetic and environmental circumstances) and the impossible lies what is possible. "[S]uspension is creative projection, i.e., making-possible" (Gelven, 2000, p. 16). Being suspended is a source of suspense and surprise. As parents we can be surprised by the intense joy, as well as by the pain, of parenting. Good parenting makes it possible for (enables) children to become their true selves, to develop a good character. Reciprocally, the cumulative work of good parenting contributes to refining the character of the parents. "[G]oodness usually seems to require a selfless or even self-sacrificing quality" (Gelven, 1997, p. 126). Selflessness and self-sacrifice are of the essence of good parenting.

In *Reason for Hope: A Spiritual Journey*, ethologist Jane Goodall (1999) grounds our human suspension in our past evolutionary heritage and our continuing cultural and, above all, moral evolution.

> So here we are, the human ape, half sinner, half saint, with two opposing tendencies inherited from our ancient past pulling us now toward violence, now toward compassion and love. Are we, forever, to be torn in two different directions, cruel in one instance, kind the next? Or do we have the ability to control these tendencies, choosing the direction we wish to go? (Goodall, 1999, p. 143)

Her answer to this last question is a resounding yes. Contrary to Kagan's argument for the power of our genetic traits in influencing our daily lives, Goodall believes that "we really do have the ability to override our genetic heritage. Like strict [firm and steadfast] parents or schoolteachers, we can reprimand our aggressive tendencies, deny them expression, thwart those selfish genes. . . . In point of fact most of us discipline those rebel genes on a day-to-day basis" (Goodall, 1999, pp. 144–45). Goodall reminds us that the great saints and spiritual leaders have demonstrated their capacity to transcend the constraints of their familial upbringing and cultural influences, and thus have expedited the progress of our moral evolution.[7] She then extends the challenge to all of us to play some role, in our own uniquely individual and collective ways, in hastening our cultural and moral evolution and thus altering the course of human destiny.

> Our task, then, if we would hasten our moral evolution, progress a little more quickly toward our human destiny. . . . We will have to evolve, all of us, from ordinary, everyday human beings—into saints! Ordinary people, like you and me, will have to become saints, or at least mini-saints. . . .

Throughout every second of every day there was change abroad in the world, change due to the impact of mind on mind; teacher and pupil, *parent and child,* world leader and citizen, writer or actor and the general public. Yes, each one of us carried the seeds for change. Seeds that needed nurturing to realize their potential.

I had no doubt that, given time, we humans were capable of creating a moral society. . . . But we did not have the luxury of millions of years to become true saints. . . . So, I thought, we would simply have to try, each and every one of us, to become just a little bit more saintlike. That, surely, we could do. (Goodall, 1999, pp. 200, 203; emphasis added)

According to psychohistorian Lloyd deMause (1974), parenting, too, has undergone an evolution in the history of Western society. Child-rearing modes have evolved from infanticidal, to abandonment, to ambivalent, to intrusive, to socialization, and finally, to helping, a mode which is just beginning to emerge. Of course, not everyone appropriated these child-rearing modes in any given historical period. For instance, even though socialization is the predominant mode of child rearing today, other modes are still practiced. DeMause (1974) describes the helping mode in the following fashion:

[B]oth parents are the child's servants, and strive to interpret the child's conflicts, provide stimulation and objects for its growing emotional needs, tolerate its regression, and in general produce a strong, independent, gentle, sincere and happy individual. (p. 54)

When Jane Goodall (1999) became a mother, she found that her mothering was influenced and guided by her own mother, by Dr. Benjamin Spock, and by her own observations of chimpanzee mothers, and "mother nature."

Most important, the chimpanzee observations suggested, was the *character* of the mother, the nature of her relationship to her infant and, to some extent, with other individuals in her community. Mothers who were . . . playful, affectionate, tolerant, and above all supportive, seemed to raise offspring who, as adults, had good relaxed relationships with community members. . . . It seemed, too, that mothers who had relaxed relations with other adults and who were assertive and confident . . . provided their offspring with a better start in life. (pp. 88–89; emphasis added)

Briefly, then, her observations of chimpanzee mothers taught Goodall (1999) that "a secure childhood was likely to lead to self-reliance and independence in adulthood" (p. 88). Another thing she learned from watching chimpanzee mothers with their infants was that "having a child should be *fun*" (p. 87). She further comments on the parenting part of her "spiritual journey" by mentioning that "there was not much time for consciously *thinking* about the meaning of life, but every day I was *feeling* the meaning of life" (p. 87). She adds, "[w]e all need, as adults, some experience to make us look at the world again through the eyes of a child" (p. 87).

The family into which children are, hopefully, welcomed to the world constitutes their first moral community. In this home, parents serve as moral models and existential mentors to their children. They model for and mentor their children on how to be good persons, how to live well, how to become fine or refined human beings, and how to achieve nobility in character. Day by day, in small and sometimes big ways, they are challenged to display mini saintlike behavior to their children. Each step we take in the direction of refining our parenting practices contributes to the overall evolution and progress of our moral society.

As has been demonstrated in the first part of the introduction, the idea of "good-enough" parenting has become alluring and pervasive in our culture. It aims at countering the apparently prevalent tendency of many so-called overly conscientious and guilt-ridden parents toward perfectionism. Many psychologists believe that when this tendency toward perfectionism becomes habitual, it is a sign of neurosis. Parents are therefore cautioned against setting excessively high standards in their attempt to become good parents. These same psychologists do not specify the parameters of "good-enough" parenting. More importantly, they have confused the critical distinction between the natural and healthy tendency of human beings to strive toward and to be inspired by the idea of excellence or perfection and the potentially neurotic tendency toward perfectionism. Moreover, perfectionism, which is ultimately a self-centered preoccupation, is a symptom of the failure to properly love and be loved; whereas, the idea of perfection in general and perfect parenting in particular inspires us to love properly (that is, selflessly).

In the absence of the struggle toward perfection, the idea of good-enough" parenting can serve as a source of consoling complacency for many parents. Consequently, poor parenting practices may be rationalized away by the comforting notion that nobody is perfect and to be human is to be imperfect. It is one thing, however, to use imperfection as an excuse for perpetual parenting failures in proper loving and another to allow the natural tension between our imperfection on the one hand and our gravitation toward perfection on the other hand to act as a spur for becoming better parents in particular and better persons in general. Guided by the inspiring insights of Iris Murdoch (the subject of chapter 3), the assumption is made that movement toward perfection is simultaneously movement toward goodness. Murdoch's moral philosophy will be applied to our understanding of what it means to be good and loving parents. The idea of perfection, which is one of the guises of goodness, inspires us to love our children properly and our proper loving of our children makes us even more good parents. Being and becoming unselfishly loving go hand in hand with being and becoming good persons. Love and goodness are almost identical, but not quite. Whereas there is no deformed version of goodness, there exists a deformed type of love which is selfish. However, if we keep in mind unselfish love, then we can equate love with goodness for our practical purposes. Thus, a constant reference is made to good *and* loving parents.

In order for children to become good and loving human beings, they need to be loved and cared for not only by parents but also by an increasing number of persons who come in contact with them, formally and informally, in family, school, community, and other societal settings. This book will focus primarily on the structure of loving and being loved in the context of parenting and being parented. In the process of being loved, children acquire the capacity to love. They, therefore, need to be loved and be able to love in order to become good and responsible citizens of the communal society of which they are to be a vital part of the whole.

The ultimate aim of this book is to provide an understanding of parental love as an ideal limit that will inspire a movement toward better parental practices. Ideas can have consequences. The idea of perfect (good) parenting is a worthy ideal toward which to aspire. It has the power to move us toward being and becoming more mature lovers of our children. As our love for our children becomes more refined and purified, we, along with our children, become better persons who embody and enact more of the goodness in life. The beauty, inno-cence, purity, perfectibility, and simplicity (which along Murdochian lines are themselves guises of goodness) of children, at least in the eyes of their parents, when properly attended to, can serve to purify and refine parents' love for their children. They can provide parents with the necessary good energy needed for meeting the endless challenges of loving parenting. Good energy is needed to counter the ever-present bad energy which is naturally fuelled by parents' self-centered concerns and children's egocentric and unlovable ways.

One introduction to the good life is through good parenting. Parenting can therefore be viewed as a spiritual practice. It is a training in selfless loving. It can teach parents to love their children for themselves and not as extensions of the parents to be grasped and bent into shape according to their own egocentric desires. Good parenting is at the same time parenting for the good, the good of (in) children, the good of (in) parents, and the good of (in) society.

The proper love of children requires responsible responsiveness to their needs. This is one way of defining the *caring* dimension of love. (This is the subject of chapter 2.) To love children is to take care of their essential needs. However, to love children requires their preparation to meet societal needs, demands, and expectations. Moreover, upon closer inspection, in human experience, needs turn out to arrange themselves along bipolar lines. Parents find themselves having to find a balanced way of meeting needs that are on opposite ends of a continuum, such as dependence versus independence. (This is the subject of chapters 1 and 2.) In chapter 1, Erik Erikson's psychosocial theory of human development will be used to illuminate the effort to understand the meaning of good and loving parenting. In chapter 2, Heinz Kohut's insights into the essential human needs required for optimal psychological growth will be applied to the parenting context. In chapter 3, Harper Lee's fictional work, *To Kill a Mockingbird*,* will be examined to illustrate extensively the application of the insights of Iris Murdoch's moral philosophy to the apprehension of what it means to be good and loving parents.

Good parenting, as an ethical human endeavor, will inevitably lead to the formulation of a pre-reflective or reflective existential understanding of life. The issues that are faced and the dilemmas that are confronted in the process of parenting raise questions about the fundamental nature of human living. Consciously or unconsciously, parents, and in turn children, struggle to come to terms with what it means to be both good and bad persons. This existential struggle in being good and bad will be the subject of chapter 4. Acknowledging and embracing our badness, while, to whatever degree possible, keeping this dimension of our existential nature in check, is an essential way of modeling goodness to our children. More concretely, chapter 4 will explore the contribution of parents to the character development of their children. Parents cannot contribute optimally to their children's achievement of good character without confronting the goodness and badness of their own character. This exploration will be pursued in the light of the insights of the existential philosopher Michael Gelven. Once again, Harper Lee's classic novel will be used as a vehicle for applying the insights of Gelven to our understanding of what it means to be good *and* bad parents. Chapter 5 will present a view of good parenting based on Rollo May's existential model of human development. Chapter 6 will conclude with a view of parenting from spiritual perspective, based once more on the work of Michael Gelven.

---

*See the appendix for a detailed description of the story of *To Kill a Mockingbird* interpreted in the light of its relevance for understanding the meaning of good parenting. The reader who is not familiar with this fictional story is advised to read the appendix before reading chapters 3 and 4.

1
Growth in Parenting

Why be good and loving parents?[1] Evolutionary psychology gives us one answer. We have been naturally selected to evolve into becoming selfishly unselfish toward our kin. We are biologically driven to selectively care for our children because we blindly want to perpetuate our genetic heritage into the future. Thus, we hear talk of the "selfish gene." Variations in our genetic makeup coupled with environmental triggers, or their relative absence, can account for the difference in the degree with which parents care for their children. All things being "normal," parents are instinctively ready to respond to the needs of their children for nourishment, nurturance, safety, security, survival, and, ultimately, self-sufficiency, which will enable them to carry on the generational continuity. Early faulty responsiveness to these needs will undermine their later potential for generative parenting.

Erik Erikson's psychosocial theory of development provides us with an answer that is compatible with that of evolutionary psychology.[2] According to his theory, human beings have two interrelated universal, biologically based needs: the need to be needed and the need to be generative—to create something and to care for one's creation which may serve the purpose of outliving the self. Even very young children thrive when they feel needed within a family. They feel both connected to other family members and individually competent when their input and contributions are welcomed and valued in the planning and execution of family decisions, activities, and projects. For Erikson, one of the avenues through which the need to be needed is optimally met is through generative parenting. The word "generativity" has special multiple meanings to Erikson. We generate (procreate) not only children, the coming generation, but also ideas, products, and even relational selves. To be truly generative, we need to care for that which we generate. Children need to be taken care of before they can become generative and take care of themselves and others, before they become productive and creative in the cultural world to which they belong and in which they feel needed.

From an Eriksonian viewpoint, preparation for generative parenting begins in infancy and continues on to young adulthood. During this period of preparation, developing persons, who are always embedded within a helpful and humanizing or harmful and dehumanizing historical and cultural context, are faced with the endless task of coming to terms with the polar dimensions of their psychosocial existence. Prepared parents, who themselves have been readied for parenting and nonparenting tasks of life through the caring mediation of their own parents and multiple other figures, real and even fictional, help their children resolve the inevitable tensions experienced by them between unfolding oppositional or contrasting individual needs and societal demands. Generative parents, directly through teaching, coaching, and guiding or indirectly through modeling, creating a supportive space, and providing access to resources and opportunities, assist their children in finding points of integrative balance between the following oppositional or contrasting needs, regardless of their time of surfacing or resurfacing: the need to trust versus the need to mistrust; the need to be autonomous versus the need to be dependent; the need for initiative taking versus the need for passive receptivity; the need for competence versus the need for knowledge of limitations; the need for selfing ("identi-fication") versus the need for unselfing ("disidenti-fication"); the need for intimate merger with an Other versus the need for self-awareness; the need for generativity versus the need for ungenerative moratorium (the need for a time-out from the call of generativity). When viewed from the perspective of the socializing agents of any given (sub)culture, these needs can be described as demands, challenges, or expectations.

Children need to securely attach themselves to trusted and consistent caregivers they can dependably rely on to meet their physical, safety, security, love and belongingness, esteem, and self-actualization needs.[3] Parents, guided by an image of perfect parenting, which is both ethically universal and culturally local, want to build a loving attachment to their children and expect their children, in order to protect and prepare them for the contingencies of life, to learn to know whom to trust and mistrust. Parents, however, do not want their children to be excessively trusting or mistrusting of others. Parents teach their children, directly or indirectly, that there is a graduated range between trust and mistrust and that where one places oneself in this range co-relates to the level of familiarity and the quality of attachment one has with the object of one's trust or mistrust. Depending on the quality of their early attachments to primary caregivers, children's trusting or mistrusting orientations can develop into character strengths or weaknesses. Children who trust too much are likely to be naïve, vulnerable, and easily manipulated by others who are not well-meaning. Children who are excessively mistrusting are likely to experience interpersonal difficulties that can lead to alienation, isolation, and possibly hostility and violence toward others.

As they grow and mature, children want to become more and more independent and to take care of themselves. At the same time, they experience the tension produced by the opposite wish to be taken care of by their caregivers. They want to hold on to their privileged dependencies on their parents. Letting go of the wish to be taken care of is never easy. Self-sufficiency brings with it increasing burdensome responsibilities. To prepare children for their future roles as responsible adult citizens, parents and other agents of the (sub)culture encourage children to become progressively more autonomous and self-sustaining. (Sub)cultures differ in the degree of their emphasis on the attainment of early autonomy and the degree to which they tolerate and even encourage the prolongation of dependency in children. There is an optimal ratio or point of balance between the encouragement of (early) independence and the nurturance of (inter)dependence to be striven for in any given caring context which needs to take into account not only the age, temperament, unique individuality, and maturity of children, but also the dominant values of the (sub)culture. Excessive needs for independence and the lurking opposite dependency needs are marks of character weaknesses. The acquired capacities for relative self-sufficiency and interdependency can become character strengths. The ability to flexibly move back and forth between roles that require independence and roles that require dependence is also a lifetime character strength.

Propelled by their emerging propensities toward imagination, playfulness, and story listening and telling, preschool children initiate and partake in imitative and creative dramas and games based on what they see and hear in their familial and (sub)cultural worlds. These imaginative activities are guided by the spirit of purposive nonpurposiveness. They serve the purpose of preparing children for the future by allowing them to project themselves into adult roles. They are simultaneously nonpurposive in that they can be nonsensical activities enacted for fun, laughter, humor, silliness, and their playful element. Parents respond to their children's imaginative initiatives with approval and praise. They may even become enthusiastic participants in their children's creative games and dramatic plays. Parents also mediate the natural cyclical oscillation of their children between active initiative taking and passive learning and following. In a creative and carefree familial space, children achieve balanced rhythmic cycles between these two modalities of being in the world. In the absence of proper caring contexts, such as authoritarian or permissive homes, children's initiatives can degenerate into either intrusive initiatives that violate the privacy or rights of others or into inhibited passivity that stifles children's sense of freedom, agency, creativity, and playfulness.

Children of the elementary school age are naturally inclined to learn and master the valued skills and technological tools of their culture. Parents, teachers, and other agents of culture are eager to teach them to become competent in understanding the logic and in making practical use of these tools and skills. Through direct instruction and modeling, children learn to figure and make things in a systematic, orderly, and methodical manner. Through participating in the pragmatic reciprocal roles of apprentice and mentor, children learn that complex skills are manageable and perfectible and that the learning of these skills has practical consequences and is instrumental for their future success. Children of this age need continuous positive feedback on their progress in mastering these valued methods and techniques. Children also learn to attempt to perfect the valued skills of their (sub)culture by competing and cooperating, playfully and seriously, with their peers, with or without adult supervision. Whether in playing games or doing school projects, children are naturally driven to both cooperate and compete with their age-mates. By participating in multiple contexts in which the learning and perfecting of valued skills is occurring, children are discovering their strengths. This is central for their identity formation. In other words, children of this age tend to tie their emerging identity to their comparable concrete competence. Parents and other cultural agents such as teachers, coaches, and other instructors play a special part in helping children discover these interests and strengths. This involves being selectively attuned to children's aptitudes, interests, and potential competencies and finding the appropriate contexts for their actualization. Above and beyond learning to become competent in the mastery of certain valued skills and tools, children need and must learn to acquire the right attitude toward work. Qualities such as being conscientious, disciplined, industrious, persistent, persevering, task oriented, and productive must be encouraged. Parents themselves need to embody these attributes children are ready to absorb. Overly competitive and overly involved or unambitious and uninvolved parents create contexts that make it difficult for children to resolve the experienced tensions between their orientations toward their own competence and incompetence. A natural sense of competence can easily degenerate into a kind of compulsive competence, where children view work as an obsessive obligation and their only criterion of worthwhileness. They center their identity too one-sidedly on their pursuit of perfectionism and success in an area of competence. Perfectionistic, critical, or negligent parents engender in their children feelings of inferiority even in areas of potential or actual competence, let alone areas of limitations and incompetence. When children acquire a healthy sense of competence, they come to feel good about themselves. They experience a kind of humble pride in their accomplished area of competence. They have a feeling of tolerance toward those who display incompetence in areas in which they are competent. They also have a feeling of admiration toward those who demonstrate competence in domains in which they are not competent. They feel a humble acceptance of their limitations in those areas in which they are aware of their incompetence. These are requirements in the making of good persons.

Selfing, acquiring a sense of who one is, and unselfing, renouncing aspects of who one is, are complementary and lifelong processes in the making of identity. Although the construction of the self begins early in childhood and continues on through the life cycle, it becomes pivotal during adolescence and young adulthood. This is in part due to the dramatic changes that occur during this period which trigger in adolescents a self-consciousness and a graduated sense of reflexivity, the capacity to stand back and reflect upon the self. It is also in part due to increased familial and societal demands, expectations, and pressures that are directed toward adolescents and which aim at preparing them for the assumption of adult responsible roles. Paralleling these parental and cultural expectations, adolescents experience the intensification of earlier needs and the surfacing of new ones. Spurred by physical, intellectual, and emotional changes, adolescents experience a qualitatively different need for affiliation, fidelity, and belongingness than they have experienced before. Their felt sense of incompleteness propels them to seek completion by way of seeking peers and, later, ideologies to attract their loyalties. The family has been the adolescents' primary source of affiliative fidelity and the center of their familial identity. But now, through the enactment of mutual loyalties with peers who are similarly needful, they acquire a peer identity. It will be some time, a process which will involve conscious and reflexive or unconscious unselfing, before they are able to coordinate these different identities as part of a larger interpersonal identity. Meanwhile, they will inevitably experience conflicting and contradictory ways of being with adults and peers. Parents who understand this transitional lack of sameness and continuity in the presentations of the adolescent self are likely to be more patient and tolerant. For a while adolescents are not aware that they may be different persons in different interpersonal settings. They lack the reflective distancing necessary for such awareness. They react differently in the presence of parents and peers because they envisage different expectations and anticipate competing and conflicting claims. That is why they may act awkwardly when they are in the presence of both parents and peers at the same time. Nevertheless, it is in the context of cultivating their adolescent friendships, which are more egalitarian than their relations to their parents, that they can refine and perfect the virtues of accuracy, authenticity, conviction, devotion, dutifulness, fairness, genuineness, loyalty, sincerity, and truthfulness. Their capacity for discerning the character of others is sharpened. They learn to modulate their antagonistic, impulsive, and competitive sentiments in the service of preserving and enhancing their affiliative fidelities. They become more attuned to the interests, feelings, and needs of their friends. They want to be liked, approved, and thought well of by them. They want to live up to their mutual obligations and expectations. The character weakness that may emerge here is that they may become excessively preoccupied with how they appear in the eyes of their friends to the point of sacrificing the integrity they have cultivated at home. Here, creative loyalty degenerates into destructive loyalty. Fidelity to friends defines what is right and good. They come to see themselves primarily through the eyes of selective others. Without the confirming eyes, ears, and mouths of these essential peers, they feel isolated, lonely, and groundless. Another related danger is that they can come to equate identity with appearance. "I am what I appear to be: the stylish clothes I wear, the car I drive, the house I live in, etc." This dangerous equation needs to be countered by parents, teachers, and other agents of culture through emphasizing values that go beyond appearances. At the same time, parents need to be tolerant and understanding of the self-conscious sensitivity of adolescents during this transitional phase to how they, and even loved ones, appear in the eyes of others. Yet another danger exists for adolescents who, having acquired a fragile sense of familial fidelity, are unable to establish and nurture mutual loyalties with peers. Thus they may tend to become either interpersonally alienated, withdrawn, and self-destructive or manipulative and destructive of others.

The felt sense of incompleteness of late adolescents and young adults drives them to search for ideologies in which to believe. The family has been the main source of their ideological fidelity and the center around which their ideological identity has been constructed. With the expansion of their intellectual, social, and moral horizons, they experience a readiness for the revision of their ideological identity. Ideology refers to the ideas (beliefs and values) and ideals that individuals identify with and want to live by. An ideological outlook defines what is good and evil, right and wrong, true and untrue, and natural and unnatural. An ideological orientation offers some answers to life's basic and ultimate questions. Late adolescents and early adults are struggling to make up their ideological minds. It is not a coincidence that idealism has been ascribed to the youth. They are ready to renounce at least part of the ideologies that they absorbed in childhood and appropriate a new configuration of ideals to live by. They may also experience conflicts and contradictions between the ideologies of childhood and the new ideologies they are attempting to appropriate. Although their actions may not match their newly declared ideology, they are prejudicially attuned to the hypocritical ideological stances of their parents or other representatives of institutions of authority. They can be so mesmerized by their ideological outlook that they fail to take into account its realism. Their need for a higher and deeper ideological loyalty is matched by the societal need to impart its ideology to its youth. The adult roles and responsibilities that young adults are encouraged to adopt are laden with ideologies. When young adults commit themselves to a religious faith, a political viewpoint or system, a vocation, or a gender role, they are at least implicitly extending their loyalties to certain ideologies. Conflicting and contradictory ideologies confuse or trivialize the potential coherence and integrity of their ideological identity. Coherence and consistency across ideologically laden roles and responsibilities contribute to integration of their evolving identity. Late adolescents and young adults are typically eager and ready to assume roles and responsibilities that make them feel they are becoming a part of the adult world of responsible citizenship. Parents and other representatives of their (sub)culture provide the opportunities, the resources, and the support needed for their pursuit of meaningful and practical adult life projects. Although the latitude for experimentation varies, depending on the socioeconomic realities of any given family, adolescents and young adults are allowed relative leeway for reflecting on or trying out different ways of life and of (potentially) making a living. Institutions of higher education can serve as a caring context in which such ideological experimentation can take place. They can be instrumental in significantly satisfying college students' intense desire for ideals. They can awaken in these young persons their sense of social responsibility and prepare them to become a part of a larger societal whole. Uncaring or selectively caring contexts, which, overtly or covertly, are driven by prejudicial ideologies such as sexism, racism, or ethnocentrism, may disallow certain groups of young individuals of the resources, opportunities, and support needed for the exploration and pursuit of appropriate and meaningful value-laden adult roles and responsibilities. This amounts to the foreclosure of possibilities for a large section of the youth population. Parents need to be aware of how their own prejudicial ideologies can close off the future possibilities potentially open to their own children. A patriarchal ideology, for example, can have a detrimental effect on what the future will hold for their adolescent daughters.

Lacking the acquired resilience necessary to tolerate the inevitable tension experienced in the selfing-unselfing-reselfing process, some adolescents prematurely foreclose their ideological identities by adopting, wholesale, without personal reflection and evaluation, their parental, ethnic, racial, political, or religious ideology. The potential for creative ideological fidelity as a character strength is forsaken. Instead, it degenerates into destructive ideological fidelity. This type of loyalty is typified by exclusivity, rigidity, inflexibility, and lack of tolerance toward that which is ideologically different. Such foreclosure in ideological identity, individually or collectively, can easily produce a predisposition toward antagonistic encounters with other individuals or groups perceived as threateningly different.

Whereas the predisposition toward ideological foreclosure and rigidity may have its origin in authoritarian child-rearing practices, the tendency toward ideological fluidity may have its roots in permissive or uninvolved parenting practices. Adolescents who are characterized by a fluid ideological outlook lack an inner valuational structure or foundation to creatively modify and build on. Their valuational stances are easily influenced by changing impulses, moods, and contextual circumstances. They are alienated from the innermost human need to discover trustworthy values to live by.

Whereas late adolescents and early adults are caught up in the struggle of finding an integrative point of balance between, on the one hand, not foreclosing their identities too soon and, on the other hand, not being lost in a fluid identity for too long, while engaged in the process of affirming and repudiating old and newly acquired interpersonal and ideological identifications, maturing adults must come to terms with the tensions aroused by the bipolar needs of other-care and self-care. Generative or selfless caring is the optimal form of other-care.[4] Generativity encompasses whatever adults generate (procreate, create, re-create, produce, or help produce) and is motivated by the evolutionary-based human need to be needed. Caring is the expanding concern for that which is to be cared for. Although adults generate products and ideas, the generation of the next generation is of primary concern for the Eriksonian model. Generative adults are ever widening their concentric circles of care to include all future generations. They care not only for their own and related families but, ultimately, for the human family. They have come to have a deep and abiding concern for the welfare of future generations everywhere. This does not mean, however, that generative parents do not care more deeply for their own children than children personally unknown to them. Generativity allows for degrees of graduated care. It disallows exclusive "pseudospeciated" caring.[5] Furthermore, in general, all adults have the potential, directly or indirectly, to become generative regardless of whether or not they are biological parents.

Paralleling the experienced tension between the need to care for the other and the need to care for the self, there exists a correlative tension between the need for a transcendent, universal, and inclusive identity and the need for a conventional and exclusive (pseudospeciated) identity. Stated differently, inclusive generative care allows for the emergence of a transcendent identity that appropriates a universal ideology. A transcendent identity is one that resonates to the universal human values expressed in the teachings and the parables of historical figures, such as Socrates, Buddha, and Jesus. These and other historical figures, along with current fictional or real ideologically inspiring models, offer new generations ideal images and pictures of human perfectibility to live by and aspire to. Even Erikson himself can be viewed as a generative model. Observe his amendment of the Golden Rule: "Do unto others that which will strengthen them by developing their best potentialities." This universal value-laden rule embodies the principle of mutual activation, without which generative caring is not possible. As social human beings, we participate in a network of mutually influencing relations in the context of which we mutually recognize, affirm, regulate, actuate, and enliven each other. Of course, this principle has its negative counterpart in mutual negation. In other words, we can bring out the best and the worst in each other. In any human encounter, to a larger or lesser degree, we are destined or condemned to influence each other, for better or for worse. In an optimal human encounter, we are required to approach our interplayer with an active and giving attitude. We are to view our interplayer as inviolate and unique. We are to regard our interplayer, as a variation on our own humanity (another me), with a benevolent gaze. The primordial inner human voice of the other calls us, especially in strange and unfamiliar situations, thus: (1) *Don't harm or hurt me, for I am another you;* (2) *Be kind to me, for I am another you.*

Generative adults who, relatively speaking and in varying degrees, have achieved transcendent (inclusive) identities continue to struggle with containing and controlling their exclusive patriarchal, political, national, ethnic, religious, racial, and familial identifications. They remain in touch, more or less, with inner tensions that are a byproduct of their previously described polar needs. They are aware of but not overwhelmed by their contradictions. Their caring orientation allows them to juxtapose the best and worst in themselves (their higher selves and their lower selves), experience humility as a result, and derive renewed energy to better themselves. They are able to take care of themselves without becoming self-absorbed or self-obsessed. They can accept the care of others without becoming demanding or dependent. By overcoming their self-centeredness, they are enabled to contribute, in small or large ways, to the developmental realization of their family, community, society, and humanity. Their selfless caring is the source of their relative integration and integrity.

Generative adults are capable of mature loving.[6] They are able to establish, maintain, and enhance intimate relations with an essential other that requires mutual devotion in spite of the frictions that they may experience as a result of differences or divisions in role functions. They have the capacity to merge their identities without fear of losing their sense of independence and separateness. They can commit themselves to each other and abide by these commitments in spite of the limitations these commitments impose on their freedoms. They can be dependent on and yet independent from each other. It must be remembered, however, that the acquisition of the capacity for love is based on the attainment of the earlier strengths of interpersonal and ideological fidelity, instrumental competence, initiative, autonomy, and trust. For example, by competently doing things for each other, devoted partners can demonstrate their love for each other in concrete ways. By allowing each other the freedom to envision and pursue genuinely valued goals without making each other feel guilty and fearful, devoted partners will find purpose and meaning in what they do in life. Devoted partners attain a balance between freedom and limits: freedom within limits. They come to the realization that the love they gain is worth the limits they impose on themselves. In spite of moments of doubt and uncertainty, they have the feeling that their margin of choice-making power is, for the most part, strengthened and not compromised. They feel that they choose to restrain themselves freely. Loving and caring partners have trust in each other. They have faith that in the context of their relationship, their innermost hopes and wishes will be attained, in spite of the dark and unpredictable dimensions of their lives together. In short, the love they have for each other brings out the best and modulates the worst in each other. It makes the inevitable tensions between them tolerable. Love makes fairness possible and thus awakens and intensifies the lovers' ethical sensibility.

Generative adults are capable of some degree of insight and foresight. They are able to see into (in-sight) themselves and their situations simultaneously. They have some understanding of their tension-producing basic needs that direct their motivations and emotions. They also have a good intuitive understanding of the motives and emotions of others and their underlying needs. They are always careful not to neglect situational and other contextual factors in their apprehension of themselves and others. They maintain a vigilant attitude toward the correctness of their value-laden assumptions that guide their understanding of themselves and others. Generative adults, to a certain degree, see ahead (have foresight) in that they anticipate, with some accuracy, the potentialities and limitations of others and the impact of their actions on others, of which they are accepting. Such responsible insight and foresight, which are the hallmarks of continually emerging wisdom, deepen the generative adults' faith in life and fellowship and heighten their ethical sensibility.

If one of our basic human needs is the need to be needed and if another interrelated need is to be generative (to selflessly care for that which we generate), then it follows that when we are engaged in other-care, we are simultaneously engaged in self-care. By meeting the needs of (essential) others we are, paradoxically, meeting our own needs. We do not pursue the care of others in order to meet our own needs. Guided by our generative drive, our primary orientation is toward the care of others. We also have a biologically based need to preserve, protect, and enhance our own needful selves. We have a natural need to take care of ourselves and what we consider our own kin and kind. The need for other-care and self-care are experienced at times as synchronous, complementary, and mutually inclusive, and at other times as conflictual, contradictory, and mutually exclusive. Optimal self-care strengthens our generative drive to care for others. Excessive and exclusive preoccupation with taking care of ourselves and what is ours can easily degenerate (de-generate) into pseudospeciation ("My kin and kind are better than and different from your kin and kind"), narcissism, distantiation, (a. being distant, separate, and isolated from others; b. keeping others at a distance from ourselves and what is ours), and stagnation. The degeneration of self-care into egoism, self-absorption, self-indulgence, mental, emotional, or physical deformation, cruel and destructive exclusivity, the avoidance of intimate contacts, the compulsive seeking of pseudointimacy with others, and a general sense of personal impoverishment is related to the failure of other-care.

As alluded to before, there are multiple pathways for the ever-widening circles of other-care. According to the Eriksonian model, our psychosocial development and growth, our relative attainment of integration and integrity is contingent on, given our strengths, limitations, resources, and opportunities, our onward and outward inclusive movement across the widening circles of care. Regardless of the pathways of care we choose, the ability to move through the expanding concentric circles of care is an essential prerequisite for moral development and personality integration. Therefore, even though generative parenting is the focus of this book, generative parents need to model for their children their ability to widen their domains of care.

Still, one primary way for being and becoming generative is through caring for children.[7] Genuine caring is guided by the nature of that which is cared for. Caring parents are attuned to the age-appropriate basic needs of their children. They are sensitive to their individual temperament and evolving character. They anticipate their future needs and unfolding potentials. They constantly struggle not to burden them by passing on to them the immaturities that they have appropriated from their own parents. They aim at helping their children develop the balanced character strengths of trust, autonomy, initiative, competence, and interpersonal and ideological fidelity. Through mutual activation, parents and children bring out the best in each other. They mutually affirm, activate, confirm, re-cognize, regulate, enliven, inspire, and actuate each other. The developing strengths of the children synchronizes not only with the strengths of the parents, but also with the instrumental importance of an increasing number of essential others who arrange themselves around the children in informal and formal concentric circles of family, school, community, and society. Simply stated, caring parents in a caring community beget caring children.

2
Parenting as Care

Caring is a central part of loving.[1] To love our children is to care for them. The way we care for them says something essential about the kind of persons we are and want to become. To care for our children is to want to engender and enhance their well-being and growth. But wanting and good intentions are not good enough by themselves. We need to translate them into actions and then to see the results. Good intentions have to have good consequences.

As parents, we need to care for our children primarily for their own sake and not for our sake. We care for them as they are *and* as the kind of persons they can become optimally, given their own unfolding powers and limitations.

We care for our children because we value them, because they are very important to us. We care for them because we need to be needed by them. The need to be needed is an essential human need. When this need is significantly fulfilled, in part through caring for our children, we too are fulfilled. The benefits of caring boomerang on us. Paradoxically, in caring for our children primarily, we care for our selves secondarily. This happens naturally, organismically, and unconsciously, and not through the conscious, deliberate, and intentional pursuit of our aim to satisfy our need to be needed by our children.

We care for our children because they matter to us, because they are very dear to us, and because they are unique and irreplaceable. Through caring for them our lives are enriched with meaning. In a caring context, the gradual, reciprocal, and mutual interactions promote the well-being and growth of not only the cared-for children, but also the caring parents.

Our children are whole persons with their own unique individual styles. To deeply care for them, we need to be sensitive to their specific, individual needs. Our caring will not be genuine if we respond to our children as if they had similar needs. We need to be selectively attuned to the specific features of their situation. Being imperfect, we cannot always respond responsibly to the individual needs of our children and take into account all the aspects of their specific situation. Factors, such as fatigue, sleeplessness, hunger, self-centered anxieties, concerns and pressures, and persistent faulty parenting patterns appropriated from the past can undermine our optimal responsiveness to the needs of our children. Still, parents are caring so long as they are guided, on the whole, by the goodness within them and the ideal of goodness from without: the pull of ideal and perfect parenting.

Through our loving care, we, as parents, not only provide our children with food, shelter, a safe and secure environment, and a sense of connectedness to an ever-enlarging circle of essential others, we are not only committing ourselves, wholeheartedly, to be responsibly responsive to their unfolding and changing needs. We are, above all, committing ourselves to a very important primary, special, exclusive relationship out of which separate, whole, independent yet inter-dependent persons are going to emerge. Out of the "we-ness" of our unfolding relationship to our children, their "I-ness" will emerge. Our care, therefore, con-tains an element of concern for the kind of persons our children are going to become. Ultimately, we want them to become good persons who are inspired by the good.

We know that very small children whose basic physical needs are not adequately met, who are not lovingly gazed at, touched, smelled, kissed, and listened and responded to, suffer emotional and psychosocial impairment. Their capacity for empathy and perspective taking will be retarded.[2] Without being able to imaginatively participate in the experience and conduct of others, they will suffer moral damage. Becoming good persons is, as a consequence, an almost impossible task, barring miraculous interventions of unexpected life events.

From the beginning, all things being relatively normal, the smallness, the cuteness, and the helplessness of our children trigger our deeply felt tendency to care for them. This potential caring response contains not only the wisdom of our evolutionary heritage but also the seeds of our moral and spiritual heritage. Infants come to the world with a wired selective sensitivity to the facial features and gestures of their caregiving adults. They come equipped with the readiness to engage in face-to-face interactions with their caregivers. Parents, in turn, are ready to "fall in love" with the general and especially facial features and gestures of their children. They are eager to participate in face-to-face nonverbal and verbal communications.

The responsive gleam in the eyes of the parents affirms, on an interbodily, preverbal, and prereflective level, the children's existence, desirability, and good-ness. The gleam in the parents' eyes contains multiple meanings: "There you are!" "We are delighted that you are here." "You belong here." "It is good that you are here." Toddlers repeatedly ask their parents while playing or performing to "look" at them. The affirming gaze of the parents substantiates their presence, their "there-ness," as the wonderful generators of playful performances. Children come to see themselves as their parents see them. The children's separate and individu-ated identities gradually emerges out of this mutual intersensorial attunement, which includes sensory modalities other than vision. Mutual empathic attune-ment makes it possible for children to grow up to be individuals who are capable of empathy and who have a solid sense of who they are.

The "seeing" or "looking" of the parents, naturally, is not always empathic, mutual, or dialogal. Children derive deep satisfaction from the knowledge that they are "present" in their parents' loving eyes and ears. It matters greatly to them how they are seen, heard, and touched by their parents. They thrive on simply being gazed at with admiration and intermittent awe. The loving gaze of the parents makes them feel more alive, real, solid, and connected. Without it, they feel empty, unreal, unsubstantial, and disconnected. In its absence they wither away and feel lost.

As they grow older, small children are able to derive sustenance, nourishment, and empowerment, when physically separated from their parents, by knowing that they are pictured in their parents' minds and remembered in their thoughts. Through this loving intersensorial interaction, children come to gradually not only see themselves as they are seen by their parents by participating in interbodily empathy, but, loving their parents, they are enabled to project themselves into their parents' perspective. In the physical absence of their parents they are able, automatically and prereflectively, to imaginatively take the standpoint of the parents to guide their thoughts and actions. They are able to picture to themselves what their parents would do under such circumstances. They come to perceive themselves as inherently worthy, valuable and good. The loving look of the parents, in the context of continuous caring, makes children look at themselves not only as loved "objects," but also as enabled "subjects" who are capable of initiating meaningful performances and projects. Within this caring context, children come to feel anchored, empowered, and at home in the world.

In this atmosphere of continuing concern and support, children, naturally and inevitably, at their own level of maturity, give expression to their care and affection for their parents. They are given endless opportunities to temper their natural self-centered tendencies and to exercise their other natural capacity to imaginatively participate in the conduct and experience of essential others. They practice their impulses toward empathy, perspective taking, cooperation, reciprocity, and altruism. They learn to coordinate their will with the will of their parents, siblings, and peers. On a preverbal and verbal level, they are learning the meaning of being in a lifelong committed relationship. They learn how to coexist harmoniously; how to be comfortably and companionably, even in silence, together.

Caring parents encourage their children to participate in joint family projects and to pursue their own independent initiatives and interests. In the process, children are learning not only about their own selective interests, meaningful projects, talents and limitations, but also they are learning how to be supportive of someone else's initiatives, interests, and projects. Moreover, children's sense of connectedness to their parents is deepened and extended when they cultivate shared interests with them. Through shared interests, children enhance their similarities to their parents. They feel more connected when they are more like, more identical to their parents. The convergence between the terms "identical" and "identity" is not accidental. Satisfying their need to be similar to their parents strengthens their emerging identity. But the opposite need is also true: the need to be dissimilar, and thus different, unique, and special. Even when children imitate and identify with the parents, in an effort to be identical to them, they still can place their own unique stamp on the imitated or identified with activity or gesture. There may be a convergence in a shared interest such as reading and a simultaneous divergence in the type of reading, such as science fiction versus biography. On a prereflective and preverbal level, children are learning that when they are enveloped in caring relations, the polarities of life (the "I" versus the "we"; separateness versus connectedness) are deeply and naturally interconnected. Care connects their need for carving their own individuated identity and their need for belongingness and union with essential others.

When children's important needs are mostly met, they feel self-fulfilled, happy, and satisfied with life. They feel emotionally stable, comfortable, whole, free, and independent. They experience their world as orderly, meaningful, filled with exciting and promising possibilities and opportunities for the creative actual-ization of their interests, talents, and potentials. On the whole, they experience harmony and unity within themselves and in their world.

To care for children means to responsibly respond to their needs in an effort to promote their well-being and growth as special and separate yet interconnected individuals. But what do children need? The answer to this question has been given in a general sense in the previous pages. Self psychologists have given us a more detailed response to this critical question. They describe seven essential needs, some of which overlap with the general description already touched upon, which are important enough to outline separately.

1. Mirroring needs. To be mirrored is to be accepted, affirmed, appreciated, and recognized.[3] Children need mirroring responses from their parents or parental figures because they are critical for their evolving sense of self. Mirroring reactions evoke and vitalize their emerging sense of selfhood. They confirm children's sense of specialness, wonderfulness, and lovableness. Improper mirroring is likely to result in undermining the natural healthy growth and, ultimately, in the fragmen-tation of the evolving social self.[4] Deficient, not-enough, mirroring predisposes children to feelings of emptiness, depression, and lack of vitality. To counter their sense of worthlessness, these children may engage in extreme, negative, and faulty behaviors in an effort to seek attention and admiration from others. Of course, the negative responses of others establishes a vicious cycle that is hard to break. The other alternative for mirroring hungry children is simply to become withdrawn and devitalized. Excessive mirroring makes children feel overstimulated and flooded by fantasies of their own perfection and greatness. As a consequence, these children experience anxiety in the face of the tension-producing fantasies. These overstimulated and overly pampered children become discouraged and dependent in the face of the resistance they encounter, to their fantasy-based initiatives, from others and from the object world.

2. Idealizing needs. Prior to their desire to experience themselves "apart" from their parents, children need to experience themselves as part of their parents. They need to be a part of their parents especially when the parents are calm, nonanxious, powerful, protective, and wise. These are qualities they lack and would like to make their own, a part of themselves. Children not only need their parents, they also admire, respect, and look up to them. They naturally gravitate toward them as figures to be idealized. Cumulative experiences of idealization are essential for evoking and sustaining their emerging sense of self.

As they grow up and mature, physically, cognitively, emotionally, and psychosocially, children begin to recognize their parents' defects and imperfections. This results in their deidealization of their parents as the idealized figures in their early lives. As adolescents, they turn to their peers, to their idols and heroes of their adolescent subculture, or to figures from their cultural-religious history for their needed idealization. They may turn to caring figures in their surroundings other than their parents, such as teachers, relatives, or the parents of peers. These new figures and objects of idealization allow them to be a part of and apart from their parents. They permit them to become their own persons, sometimes at the risk of being, hopefully temporarily, overrebellious or overly conforming to the peer group or any other target of idealization and identification. Eventually, they construct their own ideals, which will subsume, in part, ideals taken from their parents and, in part, ideals appropriated and made to suit from other objects and figures of idealization. Although they are likely to reject and modify, and on rare occasions radically revolutionize, their parents' and the surrounding traditional ideals, typically, as young adults, they come to respectfully reidealize their parents. It is attributed to Mark Twain to have said that when he was an adolescent he thought his parents to be very limited and stupid, while in his twenties he realized that they had matured significantly in a span of a few years.

Children's exposure to contradictory ideals while they are growing up makes the unfolding of the natural process of idealization/deidealization/reidealization more difficult to resolve. The multiple demands and expectations of this period adds to its complexity. This is why adolescents need a "time-out" period, a time where not too much is required of them in terms of contributing to the family or the society at large. Adolescents, as "transitional" persons, not children and not yet adults, experience their responsibilities toward themselves, others, and society with deep ambivalence. On the one hand, they want to be taken care of and have fun. On the other hand, they find it humiliating not to be treated as adults who can shoulder real responsibilities. They feel that they can, given the opportunity, take care of themselves, and maybe even others, now. Thus the dilemma of adolescence can be captured by the tension between being taken care of versus taking care of oneself and others.

Young children need to appropriate images of calmness, peacefulness, and protectiveness from their parents. They need to picture their parents as all-knowing, omnipotent, and infallible. They feel safe, secure, and empowered by these images, which they cling to tenaciously even in the face, within limits, of contradictory experiences. Deidealizing adolescents discover that their parents are far from being omniscient, omnipotent, and infallible. But in this transitional period of vacillation between their desire to take care of themselves and what is theirs and their desire to be taken care of, they still need images of their parents as calm, collected, nonanxious, efficacious, protective, but not overly so, and as caring advice givers, when their advice is sought. Such images are instrumental in helping adolescents achieve a gradual integrating balance between the experienced polarities of care: taking care versus being taken care of.

When children's idealizing needs are not significantly satisfied they feel overburdened and overwhelmed from within, by their own emotions, and later fantasies and thoughts, and from without, by tension and conflict-producing painful interpersonal interactions or unexpected resistance from the objective world. They come to experience the world anxiously as a hostile and dangerous place. They lack the capacity to soothe and comfort themselves in times of stress when their parents are not around. To feel worthwhile, they may try to find others to whom they can look up to and idealize and by whom they can feel accepted. They seek refuge in ultimate rescuers who will relieve them of the burden of assuming responsibility for a fragile and vulnerable self.

3. Similarity (being identical) to essential others needs. Children need to experience a basic alikeness to their parents, and later, to siblings, peers, and other important figures, real or fictional, in their social world. Children become like their parents, relatively speaking, by imitating and identifying with them. Parents in particular, and society in general, already have an ally in children's natural readiness to be socialized, to be a like member of the human family. Deep within us we all have the need to be similar to and different from others. Pushed to its limits, the need for similarity to essential others expresses itself in the secret desire to find someone special who is just like us, who is a mirror image of us. This is why we are in awe of identical twins. We fantasize that when we finally find our psychosocial twin, we will be less alone and more deeply connected in this world.

The linguistic link between the words "identical," "identification," and "identity" is not a coincidence. We become who we are (identity), in an important part, by becoming like (identical to) essential others through imaginatively participating in their experience and action and then internalizing, making our own, their experiential-action tendencies. Our emerging whole identity is, to a large extent, the by-product of our cumulative part identifications. But the whole is other than the sum of the parts. We always place our unique stamp upon these partial identifications. We can, though with difficulty, shed off early identifications, add new ones, and thus reconfigure our whole identity. Of course we are also limited to the types of objects of identifications that are available to us when we are very small and as we grow older. We are born to these parents or parental figures, at this time and place in our cultural and subcultural history. Yet, within these parameters, there is always a leeway for a creative synthesis of our part identifications. The need for being identical to essential others goes hand in hand with the counterneed for being different from others. Coauthoring our evolving identity is a life project that involves searching for creative ways to meet these polar needs. As parents, we offer ourselves as models and guides in this endeavor.

Children are empowered by discovering out that they are similar to their parents. When they imitate their parents, in their own unique fashion, their repertoire of competent social and problem-solving behaviors is strengthened. Moreover, their imitations and identifications make them feel closer to their parents. Even simply pointing out that they look like one or both of their parents delights them. Parents need to point out the positive physical or nonphysical resemblances to their children. "You have your father's eyes." "You have your mother's sense of humor." These experiences of alikeness to their parents intensify their desire to increase their similarities through further imitation and identification. Simultaneously, children's need to be unique, special, and different ought to be reinforced by the parents. "You are exceptionally good in math; I was never good in math!" "You have a beautiful nose; you certainly do not have your father's or your mother's nose!"

When children lack this deep sense of being similar to essential others, they are likely to feel disconnected and vulnerable. Their emerging sense of self is likely to be more fragile. They are likely to feel less solidly grounded or rooted in reality. They may have an exaggerated hunger for being like others. As they grow older, they may have an excessive need to associate with others who are similar to them in appearance, opinions, and values from whom they require endless confirmation. They are less likely to be open to associating with others who are different from them. Thus, they make it more difficult for themselves to expand their horizons and allow for change and growth.

4. Self-assertion and enhancement needs. Having developed a sense of trust in their caretakers, having entered a more differentiated and enlarged social world and having become increasingly aware of their sense of separate selfhood, children experience the biologically based need to assert themselves upon the world—to exercise their willpower. Inevitably and universally, children give expression to their budding self-assertion through negativism. This activates in caregivers the desire to socialize the children through the imposition of limits, rules, and regulations. At the same time, children experience the need to imitate and identify with their caregivers to acquire some of their powers or to avoid losing or diminishing their valued care. This in turn activates in the caring adults a certain healthy sense of narcissistic pride, which propels caring parents to invest themselves judiciously in their children who are now more concretely perceived as embodying their future hopes and aspirations. Thus, the clash of counterwills is transformed into the coordination of good wills.

Children are torn, especially during periods of heightened sensitivity such as toddlerhood and adolescence, between the needs for self-assertion, independence, separation, and individuation, on the one hand, and the needs for self-negation, dependence, connectedness, and fusion, on the other hand. They need their parents' mediation and example for resolving these tension-producing polarities. Teaching children, through direct instruction and by example how to accommodate, negotiate, compromise, and cooperate is of the essence for moral development and personality integration.

In their interest for civilized and harmonious living, parents expect and demand self-restraint, self-control, obedience, and conformity from children. They also want their children to grow up to be relatively independent and self-sufficient. Children want to progressively assert their individuality and independence, while at the same time wanting to stay close and connected to their parents. They want to obey and conform because they want to become like their loving and powerful parents. They do not want to displease their potentially punishing parents. They also want to exercise their individual freedom of choice, at times indiscriminately, even if it means going against the rules and regulations of their parents.

While acquiring the capacity to juggle their way between the polarities of self-assertion and self-restraint, they alternate between selfish and unselfish states. When in a selfish state, children are egocentric, possessive, and willful. They are unable or unwilling to imagine the state of others. They are not guided in their contemplated actions by proactive feelings of shame and guilt. They may or may not experience these feelings retroactively. Retroactively experienced feelings of shame and guilt do not necessarily deter them from repeating the pursuit of their egotistic designs. Even when they are accompanied by feelings of anxiety, the self comes first. When they are driven by their selfish impulse, they can be mean, manipulative, and untruthful. Children, however, can also be driven by unselfish impulses. They can, over time, imaginatively participate in the experience and action of others. Being able to imagine the fundamental nature of others, they can show empathy and compassion.

The delicate balance between self-assertion and self-restraint can be achieved only in an atmosphere of judicious and caring parenting. These painful polarities, for parents and children, can be relatively resolved only when parents display **the four fs:** affection, fairness, firmness, and flexibility. In a home environment characterized by such positive parental attributes, children begin to feel limited, but not inhibited by the emotions of shame and guilt. These emotions become signals of self-restraint emanating from a healthy developing conscience.

Shame and guilt are moral emotions.[5] When children experience shame and guilt, they can tell the difference between right and wrong. Shame refers to the feeling of embarrassment which typically occurs in the context of being discovered by and exposed to the judging eyes of others for having failed to live up to expected standards of conduct. Guilt, which developmentally follows shame, is an uncomfortable feeling of badness for having failed to live up to inner or internalized standards of conduct. Adaptive guilt has the wishful aim of repairing and restoring one's optimal relation with others. Guilt typically requires (limited) empathy for having caused discomfort, pain, or distress to others. With adaptive guilt, children acquire the gradual awareness of personal responsibility.

Deformed parental caring undermines the development of a healthy sense of self-assertion that is balanced with a healthy sense of self-restraint. Deformed care can be a by-product of different styles of child care. Authoritarian parents emphasize obedience and inflexible discipline. Permissive parents do not know how to set fair and appropriate limits. Negligent parents are not available for their children. Inconsistent parents are erratic in the application of their discipline, limit setting, and the display of their affection. These deformed styles of child care are likely to cause children to experience either excessive feelings of shame and guilt, which result in the paralysis of children's creative self-assertion, or diminished feelings of shame and guilt, which result in children's destructive or tyrannical self-assertion. The excess or diminution of the emotions of shame and guilt cripple children's capacity for empathy, compassion, and perspective taking. They stand in the way of the objective imagination of the reality of others and in the extension of an appropriate helping hand. Whether they are hyperempathic or not empathic enough, children's vision of the world is clouded and distorted. They are still imprisoned in a self-centered, egoistic existence.

Good parenting requires the encouragement of obedience to higher authority without undermining children's emerging sense of freedom. It involves the delicate integration of the obedient self and the assertive self within a larger whole Self. Here lies one of the paradoxes of human development: to obey and at the same time to feel free, where obedience becomes (limited) freedom. An example of this is the cultivation of good habits. Initially, acquiring good habits requires following externally imposed rules and regulations. Over time, rules and regulations have the potential of becoming internalized and serve as the source of creative life projects and healthy lifestyles. Whether it is related to the learning of a physical, manual, musical, or mental skill, the acquisition of a good habit involves the coming together of disciplined obedience and creative freedom. Interestingly, in the process of cultivating a good habit, the focus of attention progressively shifts away from the self toward the project of interest at hand. When children are learning good habits, which provide the framework for actualizing their particular potential, they are learning self-transcendence. They are learning to go beyond their self-centeredness and become absorbed in a project of interest outside themselves. It is a process that requires unselfing. To learn a good habit (skill) is to become a good person, at least relative to the acquired area of competency and to the best of one's ability.

Developmental growth during early childhood and adolescence involves integrating self-assertion with obedience. Especially during the earlier phase of these periods of development, children can be very strong willed, headstrong, impulsive, self-centered, stubborn, insubordinate, and negativistic. Even in their language, young children make heavy use of words such as "me," "mine," and above all, "no." This kind of language gives expression to their developing independence and separate existence. Some of their verbal expressions carry moral connotations ("It's not fair"). But for them fairness may mean getting what they want. During early childhood, children will do anything to get what they want and not think anything of it. In the absence of potential punishers, they will steal, lie, be cruel to others, and more, all in an effort to get what they want, especially in those circumstances where their wishes or desires conflict with the wishes or desires of others. The psychology literature in this area, however, also shows that, in spite of their cognitive egocentrism, children of this age are capable not only of cruelty but also compassion. They can transcend their egocentrism. They can be altruistic, empathic, helpful, cooperative, sharing, sensitive to the feelings of others, and so on.[6] But of course, in all this they are limited. The point to be made here is that children, during this early period of childhood, can display contradictory moral logic. Depending on their impulse-driven mood, they can say (or think or behave accordingly) "This is mine because I want it"; "This is not mine because daddy said so and if I do not give it, I'll get it"; "This is not mine, I am going to give it to him because he is crying." Children's moral inconsistency will decrease as they integrate their impulse toward self-assertion with their impulse toward obedience. For example, within limits, five-year-old children are better able to follow the rules such as turn taking in simple games and display some self-restraint upon losing than are two-year-old children. They can tell and acknowledge the difference between "made-up truth" and "real truth."

To help them achieve a delicate balance between their selfish and unselfish predispositions, children's autonomous efforts and spontaneous initiatives are to be respected and encouraged by parents. Moral development occurs in the context of respectful mutual activation or engagement between children and their parents. Respectful affirmation of the children's self-chosen initiatives does not mean that parents allow their children to get away with murder, that children be allowed to harm or hurt themselves or others in the process. The children are to learn that respect is a two-way street. Because they are impulsive, lack self-control, and their fantasies and emotions can run wild, they need external control and firm limit setting. Parents need, on the one hand, to nurture the child's self-chosen initiatives and, on the other hand, set limits on some of these initiatives. Limit setting, however, can be implemented in a judicious manner and does not have to be harsh and authoritarian. Advancement toward goodness takes place when children are enabled and empowered to integrate and coordinate their impulse toward obedience with their impulse toward autonomy. This can only occur in a home atmosphere that embodies compassionate, judicious, and authoritative childrearing strategies.

To help children integrate their impulse toward obedience with their impulse toward self-assertion, parents face the challenge of balancing the threatening side of their authority with guiding benevolence. Children come to sense that in spite of external constraints and internal physical, emotional, and cognitive limitations, they still have a leeway for asserting their own will and pursuing their own initiatives.

When children are treated fairly and respectfully, they are enabled to achieve a balanced awareness of their privileges and obligations, of their rights and limitations. The benevolent judiciousness of parents tempers the willfulness of children and makes it possible for them to join the good will of their parents, to offer their willingness, while maintaining their own willpower. The opportunity for the rise of willfulness or its opposite, willessness, is diminished. Such judiciousness helps children develop a healthy respect for moral rules.

When children are treated with fairness and respect, they come to experience themselves as separate-yet-included persons of equal essential worth with their own voice, feelings, thoughts, and viewpoints, in spite of the differences they perceive in age, size, power and role function. Equality in worth is further fostered when children are encouraged to become cooperative and helpful participants in joint familial tasks and other family projects. Families purposefully united in familial projects and economic pursuits will nurture in children the inner freedom to move on to become eager and active participants in whatever school, play, or work setting their family or culture has ready for them. Familial support, unity, and harmony helps children bind together their impulses of self-assertion and obedience.

5. *Resistance needs.* Children need to repeatedly experience the resistance of the world of objects and persons and their own resistance to these objects and persons to feel their aliveness, solidity, and autonomy. This spirit of resistance becomes universally focal during the toddlerhood and adolescent years. To concretely experience their emerging sense of separateness and autonomy, children need to experience their parents as benign opposing forces without fear of loss of love, support, or encouragement. They need this oppositional confrontation without concern about harsh retaliation. In the presence of unnecessarily or provocatively resistant children, parents need to be, within limits, very accommodating, patient, and tolerant.

Children need to give expression to their naturally emerging oppositional stances toward the world in general and their parents in particular. Their oppositional voices need to be heard. By opposing their parents without being afraid of hurting their relationship to them, children develop stronger individual identities. They acquire a healthy sense of assertiveness. Their sense of selfhood is strengthened.

As can be surmised, what has been labeled as "resistance" needs, or what self psychologists have termed "adversarial" needs, could easily be subsumed under *independence/individuation needs.* In fact, there are psychologists who uphold that the most essential human needs can be subsumed under two bipolar needs: the need for agency or self-enhancement versus the need for communion or connectedness.[7] Regardless, it is safe to say that human needs are interrelated and are not mutually exclusive. Children's resistance or adversarial needs are intrinsically interrelated to their needs for autonomy, mastery, and separateness.

To assist children in developing a healthy sense of assertiveness, parents need to assume the role of benign adversaries with humility. A certain resilience that enables parents to absorb, within limits, verbal assaults and insults from their children is necessary. This in turn requires a degree of caring detachment on the part of the parents. It does not mean, however, that parents allow their children to step all over them. The rule of the four fs still applies: The need to be affectionate, fair, firm, and flexible. Parents hold on to what they see as right and good conduct or stance. But parents ought to let go of what they can close one eye to, without compromising their moral standpoint. Parents can bracket their egoism, minimize what is minor, trivialize the trivial, and be willing to let some things pass. This is a tall order and not an easy thing to do, especially when the raw emotions are aroused. Nevertheless, where love prevails, within the limits of human imperfection, it can be done.

Children who do not acquire a healthy sense of assertiveness, develop faulty ways of coming to terms with the interpersonal challenges in their everyday lives. One such faulty strategy is to become shy and withdrawn. Another is to engage in passive-aggressive means of getting one's way. A third may involve attributing hostile intentions to the behavior of others, where none exist, and thus taking a hostile preemptive stance. Here the best defense is a quick offense. Children may avoid asserting themselves because they are afraid of the harsh consequences or serious losses that will result. A low self-esteem is a likely by-product of a faulty sense of assertiveness. It is either "Do unto yourself what you think others will do unto you," or "Do unto others what you perceive them as contemplating doing unto you."

6. *Communion (comm-union) needs.* Self psychologists refer to this as the "merger" need. Children have a need to merge with their idealized parents or caregivers. They need to experience a state of oneness with the figures who care for them. Even adults experience the need for union with at least one essential other. Many psychologists assume that in the beginning, infants cannot differentiate between themselves and their caregivers. The boundaries of a separate sense of self are established over time. Infants, in other words, have no comprehension where they end and their parents begin. Only with experience, exploration, and experimentation, do they discover their physical (bodily) and later their psychosocial selves. An amorphous or diffused state of communion is the original experience of infants. This primordial experience forms the ground from which an autonomous self emerges through the gradual process of individuation. It is also this same early foundational experience which predisposes human beings in general and children in particular to seek union with others. This yearning for oneness with significant others is with us from our beginnings and it shows itself on different levels of integration, depending on our level of maturity. Children and adults seek to find a

balance between their need for communion and connectedness, on the one hand, and their need for separateness, autonomy, and individuation, on the other hand. This is an endless, lifelong task.

When children's need for communion with essential others is not adequately met, they lack the solid foundation on which a secure sense of selfhood is constructed. Interestingly, children (or adults) who experience loss of contact with reality are unable to hold on to the boundaries that separate their physical or psychosocial selves from their physical or psychosocial worlds. But in less severe states, communion-hungry children (or adults), in order to counter a basic lack or a sense of emptiness (a "black hole" in their innermost center), adopt maladaptive strategies for coping. To compensate for their basic lack, they attempt to achieve a pseudostate of communion through controlling or becoming possessive of others or through submitting to the control of others. Children and adolescents whose communion needs are adequately met are optimally positioned to remain securely connected with their caring parents while at the same time free to be and become their own authentic, independent selves.

7. Self-efficacy (agency) needs. Some psychologists have referred to this as the need for mastery or competence.[8] Infants and children need to become aware that their actions have effects; that they are the causes of these effects; that their efforts and initiatives have an impact on the world. They also learn that their actions have consequences, which they experience in the form of feedback from parents and the (physical or social) environment. Gradually, based on cumulative experiences involving initiatives, effects, and consequent proper feedback, children develop a sense of confidence in their competence; a belief that they are capable of carrying out actions that are required in any given situation; that they *can* meet the demands of the physical and social environment. This "I can" feeling is essential for their developing self-concept. Self-efficacy is critical for children's evolving self-esteem. Self-efficacy is instrumental in consolidating children's emerging sense of self. It is a source of empowerment and pleasure. Children delight in their accomplishments. They feel empowered by their acquired sense of agency; they are subjects who have an impact on the objects (things, persons, and events) of their world.

Children's vital sense of self-efficacy, and consequently their healthy sense of self-concept, develops from consistency, contingency (consequences are contingent upon specific actions), and regularity between children's actions and the reactions of caring parents and other essential figures in children's environment. When these elements of care, consistency, and contingency are either missing significantly or skewed, children acquire a low sense of self-efficacy and, as a result, a low sense of self-esteem.

Just as children learn that they are the agents (subjects) behind their own actions, they also become aware that they are objects of evaluation and are subjected to influences from their parents and the environment. In the context of optimal reciprocal interactions, children become cognizant of their limitations without undermining their sense of self-efficacy. They also become aware of their responsibilities toward others, which require consideration, cooperation, compromise, and contribution to the communal good.

   8. *Affective (empathic) attunement needs.* Children need their parents or caregivers to be attuned to their affective states, their emotional highs and lows, and their changing experiential states. This kind of attunement validates the subjective experiences of children. It affirms the rightness of their perceptions of themselves and their world. More than that, accurate empathic attunement helps children contain and modulate their emotional states. It assists them in regulating their emotion-laden tensions. It calms and soothes them. It restores and revitalizes their weakened sense of emerging selfhood. Through empathic attunement, parents convey unconditional acceptance as well as the uniqueness and specialness of their children. Children acquire a deep sense of their own lovability in spite of their dark urges and rages; in spite of their changing affective states (the "bad me" in contrast to the "good me"). They develop a sense of trust in the mostly reliable soothing and affirming goodness of their parents (the "good parent") in spite of the inevitable occasional empathic failures (the "bad parent"). Children are then able to soothe themselves in the physical absence of their parents. They do not find any unconscious need to compartmentalize images of themselves or those of their parents into good and bad me's or good and bad parents. They are better able to tolerate delays of gratifications and the ambiguities of life situations. They develop a basic faith in their own goodness and in the goodness of the world in spite of their own badness or the badness of the outside environment. Affective or empathic attunement, therefore, is instrumental in maintaining and enhancing children's evolving sense of self.

   Children who experience a significant history of empathic failures develop a fragile and tenuous sense of self. They are unable to regulate their own tensions, calm themselves in times of turmoil, or contain their shifting affective states. They may find it difficult to perceive their affective states accurately. They are less likely to feel at home in their bodies or in their world. They may lack trust in their own goodness or in the goodness of others. As such they perceive the outside world as a potentially hostile place. Being self-absorbed, they are less likely to be empathic toward others. This requires accurate imaginative participation in the experiences of others, which they lack. To counter their fluctuating and tension-producing experiential states or their lack of vitality, children and adolescents who have grown up in a faulty empathic environment, may engage in pseudovitalizing, high-risk activities, such as the abuse of alcohol and drugs or compulsive exercising and fasting, in order to contain their tensions or ward off feelings of emptiness, depression, and falling apart.

3
The Moral Dimension of Parenting

I ris Murdoch is a moral philosopher and a novelist who does not address herself to the issue of parenting as a moral vocation.[1] Her moral philosophy (sometimes referred to as moral psychology) does lend itself to such an extrapolation. For her, love constitutes the supreme virtue of morality. Murdoch is concerned with the critical moral questions How to be? and How not to be? especially in the context of the absence of a theistic belief system. Her answer is deceptively simple. We need to be good persons for no reason at all *and* because it is the most important thing to do, given the contingencies of our lives. Under "contingencies," are subsumed notions such as the transient nature of our lives, our sense of fragility, vulnerability, finitude, and mortality, our smallness and nothingness in the grand scheme of things, our susceptibility to chance and twists of fate, the lack of completeness and closure to our unfolding lives, and the aimlessness, formlessness, pointlessness, and purposelessness of life in general. This does not preclude us from being naturally predisposed to impose pattern and purpose on human experience. In spite of all this, we are called to be good, to play on a Christmas theme, "for goodness' sake." We need to perpetually struggle to be and become good persons because we are instinctively beckoned by the call of goodness in its various guises out there in the world: perfection, purity, innocence, beauty, and simplicity. Something in us resonates to these attributes or markers of goodness. Goodness itself remains indefinable, independent, and transcendent. We are destined to be pulled by the magnetic gravitational pull of goodness. Our imperfect souls yearn for the pursuit of perfection. Love is experienced as the tension that results from the arc that joins our imperfection with our great quest for perfection. Love is our response to the silently experienced voice: *Be ye perfect!* Love leads to goodness; goodness purifies and refines our love. We can envision perfection, and consequently, we can live our lives in the light of that vision. We can derive a good energy source from the alignment of the potential for goodness within us with the representations of the goodness out there in the world, such as the beauty in art and nature or the innocence and purity of our children or the presence of virtuous individuals. We can also derive a bad energy source from the (mis)alignment of the selfish impulses within us and the corresponding or complementary human or nonhuman forces and resources in the social and physical environment.

From a Murdochian viewpoint, the opposite of good is not evil but, rather, the absence of good. Correspondingly, the opposite of love is not hate but, rather, the absence of proper love or the presence of deformed love, which creates the conditions that make the commitment of harmful and "evilish" acts possible. When proper love is missing, we may experience rage, jealousy, self-hatred, emptiness, loneliness, self-pity, depression, or antipathy toward others. The absence of a proper loving orientation shows itself in the form of inaccurate perception. This distortion in how and what we see predisposes us to act in bad faith. We are prey to misattributions, misinterpretations, misapprehensions, or simply misperceptions. When our loving orientation is limited, our capacity to see the real, the true, the beautiful, or the good becomes limited. Our perceptions become clouded and contaminated. We no longer see our world accurately or clearly. We become inclined toward not apprehending the perspective, viewpoint, or the beingness of others. Love, reality, and truth go together. In other words, the real and the true are revealed through a proper loving orientation. Refined love unveils that which is real and true and leads to what is good. Goodness shows itself through a truthful depiction of reality, which is disclosed through love.

This abstract introduction points to the assertion that as human beings we can only become good (moral) and known through love. In the context of parenting, the more we love our children, the better we get to know them as individuals and the better persons we become. We become good through loving and being loved. This is what human beings, in their innermost hearts, desire. This may sound, at first sight, simple. Yet, from a Murdochian viewpoint, it is one of life's most difficult and demanding achievements. It is an endless task that we human beings face. Our ultimate failures are failures in love. These setbacks, however, ought not to discourage us from trying and trying again to perfect the highly moral discipline of love.

Why is it so difficult for us to love properly? The answer lies in the definition of love. Once we find out what Murdoch means by love, we understand why loving is such a formidable task. "Love is the perception of individuals." Initially, this definition appears deceptively simple and general. Upon closer scrutiny, it turns out to be a complex and highly specialized definition. The two key terms are *perception* and *individuals*. By *perception*, Murdoch means not only looking, seeing (and of course hearing, smelling, tasting, and touching, although the metaphor of vision occupies a special place in Murdoch's moral philosophy), but also apprehending or understanding as when we say "I see what you mean." To love, therefore, is to perceive (see or look at) the objects (or subjects) of our love as *individuals*—as others who are different, independent, and separate from ourselves and who have realities (minds, needs, and voices) of their own. As individuals, their differences from us and each other need to be accepted, affirmed, and maybe even cherished. Their autonomy and freedom requires our recognition and respect. We are to live with their separateness and allow them to live and be themselves. We are called upon to coexist and be tolerant of their separate realities.

In our relationships to our children, it is easy to see them as similar to and extensions of us. Similarity strengthens the attachment bond between parents and children. Exclusive or excessive emphasis on the similarity dimension absorbs children into our egoistic selves and denies them of their individuality. An imbalanced focus on sameness feeds into our natural proclivity toward self-inflating pride, selfish vanity, power-oriented possessiveness, and insatiable grasping for immortality. It is more difficult to see our children as being different, separate, and independent of us; as having minds, needs, and voices of their own. The respectful recognition of their difference from us and each other requires not only disciplined tolerance, but also valuing their separate realities and cherishing their otherness. The fictional character Atticus Finch, in Harper Lee's *To Kill a Mockingbird* (hereafter referred to as *TKM*), embodies this perceptual predisposition toward people in general and his children, Scout and Jem (aged nearly six and ten, respectively, at the beginning of the novel, the action of which is occurring during the country's Great Depression and recovery between 1933 and 1935) in particular. Atticus, a single parent and a practicing lawyer in a small Alabama town, has created, with the help of an African American cook, an ideal home for the children to grow up in. He represents for us the good (almost perfect) parent as a moral model to his children and the good (almost perfect) citizen to his community. We are told that he is the same at home as he is outside of his home. He treats his children, as he does other members of the community, with respect. He is a "gentleman" inside and outside his dwelling place. Interestingly, even in demeanor and attire he remains relatively the same inside his house as he is outside of his house. This attests to the importance of our daily habits for the maintenance of our moral consistency. He speaks and listens to his children, as he does to everyone else, as (adult) human beings of equal dignified worth. He even allows his children to call him by his first name, Atticus. It is worth noting that for Murdoch, language (everyday talk) is a very important moral medium. How we talk to each other reflects something essential about our moral fiber. There is always present the "extraverbal" in our verbal behavior. Moreover, just as the extraverbal has an influence on the verbal, our verbal transactions, at least on occasion, have a transforming impact on the quality of our everyday consciousness.

   TKM is a story about love: love in the most intimate sense (Atticus's love for his children) and love in the highest impersonal sense (Atticus's love for humanity). In a Christ-like response to his daughter's question regarding whether or not he is a "nigger lover," Atticus gives expression to the highest form of impersonal love: "I do my best to love everybody" (*TKM*, p. 108). The theme of difference (in age, sex, class, and race) is of the essence of *TKM*'s narrative on love. The moral of the story is that to love properly, personally or impersonally, is to perceive (regard) others as individuals, regardless of how old they are, what gender or socioeconomic and racial background they belong to. Atticus repeatedly urges and encourages his children to attempt to understand (see accurately) people different from themselves by attempting to adopt the point of view of these different others. After all the traumatic trials and tribulations that the children go through, the novel ends with Atticus saying to Scout, as he tenderly helps her to her bed to go to sleep, "Most people are ['real nice'], Scout, when you finally *see* them" (*TKM,* p. 281; emphasis added). The point is also conveyed to the children that underlying our differences is the common bond of our humanness. Discussing the subject of differences between people with her brother, Scout comments, "Naw, Jem, I think there's just one kind of folks, Folks" (*TKM,* p. 227). The father's moral message has been absorbed by the daughter. The father-lawyer has accepted to defend an African American man falsely accused of raping a white woman, knowing the consequences of his decision. The children attend a religious service in an African American church. Scout wants to visit the house of Calpurnia, their African-American cook. Jem invites a boy, who is from a lower socioeconomic background, for dinner to his house. Atticus converses with the boy at the dinner table on an adult-to-adult equal basis. He tells his children that even "A mob's made up of people, no matter what. Mr. Cunningham [a poor client-farmer] was part of a mob last night, but he was still a man" (*TKM,* p. 157). In his dramatic defense of his innocent client, Atticus emphasizes the importance of regarding human beings as individuals and not according to prejudicial mental schemes or categories such as race. His argument converges on the conclusion, "You know the truth and the truth is this: some Negroes lie, some Negroes are immoral, some Negro men are not to be trusted around women—black or white. But this is a truth that applies to the human race and to no particular race of men" (*TKM,* p. 204). In his home, Atticus creates an atmosphere and bodies forth a presence that allow his children to feel free to be themselves, to be "Scout" and "Jem." Under the protective but not overly protective, and guiding but not intrusive loving gaze and words of Atticus, and in turn Calpurnia, the children are allowed and encouraged to disclose and discover reality (and falsehood) and goodness (and evil). In the process they are being and becoming their authentic selves, even if it means going against traditional, misguided ageist, sexist (girls should dress and act in "ladylike" ways), socioeconomically elitist, and racial prejudices. When Scout is told by her aunt Alexandra that it is wrong to go around in "overalls" and to play and conduct oneself in an unfeminine manner, her father counters by assuring his daughter that "he didn't mind me much the way I was" (*TKM,* p. 81).

Before elucidating the structure of proper love, there are three obstacles to perceiving others as individuals, which are touched on by Murdoch, that need to be briefly described: conventional conformity, self-inflating fantasy, and destructive compensation for lack of love.

In his perception of others, Atticus refuses to be guided by the percepts of the collective Other. He resists having his judgment clouded by the opinion of the majority of his fellow citizens. "[B]efore I can live with other folks I've got to live with myself. The one thing that doesn't abide by majority rule is a person's conscience" (*TKM,* p. 105). Unlike other men (fathers), he does not carry a gun and hunt; he does not play football; he chooses to remain a single parent; and he lets his daughter run around in overalls. And when he is "chosen" to defend an innocent black man, he goes against the prejudicial sentiment of the majority by aiming to defend him in all seriousness. Unlike his sister, Alexandra, he does not adhere to the percepts of the conventional past in classifying people according to age, sex, class, and racial background. To the degree that she is a conventional conformist, Alexandra is limited in her capacity to perceive others as individuals, and thus in her ability to love.

Unlike her brother Atticus, Alexandra uses the mental classification of people in order not to perceive them as individuals. She partakes individually of the collective fantasy that because of her hereditary and religious background, she is not only different but, magically, better than members of certain other groups. This form of fantasy-based self-inflation becomes a source of false pride. Atticus, on the other hand, checks himself from even using his genetically given and acquired skills and competences, such as intelligence, education, and marksmanship, for the purpose of self-inflation and false pride. When his daughter, Scout, questions the good neighbor, Maudi, as to why her father would not take pride in his marksmanship, Maudi replies, "If your father's anything, he's civilized in his heart. Marksmanship's a gift of God, a talent. . . People in their right minds never take pride in their talents" (*TKM,* p.98). When people derive false pride from self-inflating fantasies regarding their exceptional or special worth relative to other human beings, they become oblivious to the reality of others. The more we exaggerate our self-importance through our fantasy work, the less we allow ourselves to see others, as individuals, with compassionate clarity. And these others include our own children.

Whereas Atticus Finch has created a home fit for children to grow up and thrive in, Bob Ewell, the man who accused Tom Robinson, Atticus's innocent client, of raping his daughter, Mayella, has failed miserably in constructing a home suitable for children. Like Atticus, Bob Ewell is a widowed single parent. That is where the comparison ceases. He is what Atticus is not; he is not what Atticus is. He is an illiterate man who smokes, drinks, spends his welfare checks on alcohol, uses foul language, is verbally, physically, and sexually abusive of his children, and bends or violates the law whenever he can get away with it. He is crude, cowardly, dishonest, deceitful, heartless, indecent, intolerant, irresponsible, racist, selfish, uncivilized, and unrefined in character. He is an authoritarian father who is utterly neglectful of his children's needs for food, decent shelter, safety, security, a sense of belongingness, self-esteem, and self-actualization—their need to become, given their strengths and limitations, the best persons they could become. He is unable and unwilling to provide them with a nurturing environment. Above all and in short, he fails to love them properly. Love is either totally absent or disfiguringly present. Instead of meeting his children's need for love; instead of attending to and supplying their presonal needs, Bob Ewell uses his children to meet his own selfish needs. He has succeeded in insulating, separating, and thus alienating his children from the rest of the surrounding community. He uses vulnerable others—his children and a black man—as scapegoats for his hostility, and destructiveness as a compensation for his ineptitude. The frustration of the ultimate desire, the superordinate need to love and be loved properly, creates the condition that makes the siege of sadomasochistic spirit (the tendency toward self/other destructiveness) possible.

To emphasize again, love, for Murdoch, means nonviolently perceiving (apprehending) others as individuals. The spirit of tolerant coexistence is of the essence of love. Love, however, requires a special kind of perception (seeing). To love properly is to see properly. In Murdoch's line of thinking, there is no differentiating demarcation between seeing, being, and doing; between our mode of seeing, our mode of being, and our mode of acting in the world. Proper perception has special inherent and enabling characteristics (or virtues). It is only by comprehending these characteristic components of proper perception that we come to understand the structure of proper love and why loving is such a difficult and endless task. In Murdoch's writings, some of these characteristics overlap and spill into one another. Murdoch realizes this and says that it is in the nature of moral concepts to overlap and fuse into each other. Here, an attempt will be made to keep these components separate for the purpose of simplifying as much as possible.

1. Attention

Attention is an inherent quality of proper perception. It refers to the capacity of our consciousness to concentrate or focus on something or someone. We are always, in degrees, attending or failing to attend to a person, object, or event. The target of our attention could be ourselves—our thoughts, feelings, fantasies, or imaginings. Our consciousness is always oriented toward something other than itself. Murdoch makes a distinction between improper and proper attention. Improper attention is failed or divided attention or attention that is excessively directed toward the self. When we are properly attentive, our consciousness is directed away from the self. It is wholeheartedly focused on a particular object (subject) in a particular context (situation). To be properly attentive is to direct our vision toward an individual reality without interference from our egoistic concerns, needs, or motives. It is to be focused on the objects (subjects) in and for themselves. Good attention is selectively attuned to good (excellent) external realities, such as good art, good (virtuous) individuals, our good earth (nature), or even the idea of goodness (perfection), from which we derive a good source of energy. Proper attention requires disciplined effort. It shows itself in the way we look at things and people in our everyday lives. Proper attention requires of us to be concentrated on differences and details in our physical and social environments. Goodness is to be found in the details of our worlds. What complicates matters is that, being human, we have the natural tendency to focus either excessively on ourselves or to crudely concentrate, with a clouded vision, on things, persons, or happenings that are sources of bad energy due to our egoistic anxieties or narcissistic pursuits. This does not mean that to be properly attentive we need to always focus on external realities with good sources of energy. It simply means that we constantly try to look at the good in objects and individuals, while remaining cognizant of the bad, but always seen in perspective and placed in the right context. This includes ourselves as objects of attention. To counter our natural narcissistic tendencies, we need to constantly be on the lookout—to be able, with effort, to refocus to different and new objects and sources of good energy.

Attention is a cardinal characteristic (virtue) of proper perception (love) for Murdoch. In a sense, we are what we attend to. Our habitual objects of attention come to define the kind of persons we are. To change as persons, we need to change our objects of attention. But, change, according to Murdoch, does not come about by way of a momentous act of willpower. We have some (slight) control over our objects of attention. It is the slow, small, effortful steps that we take everyday that cumulatively lead to a qualitative change over time. We decide to read this rather than that book, magazine, or journal; to talk to this rather than that person; to dwell on this and not that topic; to pursue this and not that interest; and to engage in an activity to the exclusion of another. To cultivate a refined attentive capacity and to keep it from backsliding into an ordinary and dull orientation of consciousness, we need to guard against the natural tendency to take for granted our familiar everyday transactions with the objects and persons in the world. We are to remind ourselves of their opacity and inexhaustibility. To look again and again, from different viewpoints and always ready to be surprised by the detailed difference in the light of our expectations and anticipations, is an art that requires discipline and practice. The predisposition to think that we have figured something out in advance or fairly quickly upon first or repeated sights (hearings, smells, tastes, or touching contacts) can be a major obstacle to the cultivation of refined attention.

Children, universally, need undivided attention. They come alive and thrive under the attention and admiring eyes of their parents. "Look at me!" "Listen to me!" "Watch me do this!" These are repeated demands for attention that children make of their parents. When their need for proper attention is inconsistently or repeatedly not met, children either move away or against their parents in direct or oblique ways. In *TKM*, Dill, an intelligent, imaginative, and adventurous boy, is befriended by Scout and Jem. He spends his summers with his Aunt Rachel, whose house neighbors the Finch's. Upon being abandoned by his biological father, Dill's mother remarried a young lawyer. Whereas Scout and Jem live in the fictional town of Maycomb, Alabama, Dill's home is in Meridian, Mississippi. Dill decides to run away from home and arrives, unannounced, at the Finch's home. Upon being asked by Scout why he did it, his response is that his parents "just wasn't interested in me" (*TKM*, p. 143). And, he adds,

"They stayed gone all the time, and when they were home, even, they'd get off in a room by themselves . . they didn't want me with 'em . . what I'm tryin' to say is—they *do* get on a lot better without me, I can't help them any. They ain't mean. They buy me everything I want, but it's "now-you've-got-it-go-play-with-it. You've got a roomful of things. I-got-you-that-book-so-go-read-it." Dill tried to deepen his voice. "You're not a boy. Boys get out and play baseball with other boys, they don't hang around the house worryin' their folks." Dill's voice was his own again: "Oh, they ain't mean. They kiss you and hug you good night, an' good mornin' and goodbye and tell you they love you." (*TKM*, p. 143)

In short, Dill moves (runs) away from his parents because they have failed to meet his need for loving attention. In contradistinction to Dill's home, in Scout and Jem's home, the need for proper (loving) attention is not only met but taken for granted. In response to Dill's revelations, Scout reflects:

I found myself wondering what life would be like if Jem were different, even from what he was now; what I would do if Atticus did not feel the necessity of *my presence,* help and advice. Why, he couldn't get along a day without me. Even Calpurnia couldn't get along unless *I was there. They needed me.* (*TKM*, p. 143; emphasis added)

It is clear from Scout's ruminations that when we attend wholeheartedly to a particular person, we are giving nonverbal expression to our valuing of this special person's presence and affirming this unique individual's existence. The need for attention and the need to be needed are interwoven.

In a loving home, children and parents become each other's objects (subjects) of proper attention. Proper attention is not constant and always wholehearted attention. This is humanly impossible. Moreover, children and parents need time out from each other. In the same cited dialogue between Scout and Dill, Scout remarks, "You don't want 'em [parents] around you all the time, Dill" (*TKM*, p. 143). As they grow, children require increasing privacy in order to develop an identity of their own. During their years of development, children pay attention to their parents' objects (subjects) of attention. They naturally gravitate toward their parents' objects of attention. By making at least some of them their own objects of attention, they are, through the mechanisms of imitation and identification, increasing their closeness and similarity to their parents. They are joining, participating, and appropriating their parents' worlds through the establishment of mutual objects of attention.

Reading, as an activity of interest, is a good example of a primary object of attention in Atticus Finch's home. In her first day in school, Scout tells her first-grade teacher, Miss Caroline, that her father is "so tired at night he just sits in the living room and reads" (*TKM*, p. 17). Scout reflects further: "Sometimes when we made a midnight pilgrimage to the bathroom, we would find him [Atticus] reading. He said he often woke up during the night, checked on us, and read himself back to sleep" (*TKM*, p. 57). And in comparing her father to other fathers, Scout says, "He [Atticus] did not do the things our schoolmates' fathers did: he never went hunting, he did not play poker or fish or drink or smoke. He sat in the living room and read" (*TKM*, p. 89). The activity of reading also acquires multiple functions and meanings. It serves the purpose of privacy and recuperation. The narrator of *TKM*, Scout, states, "As we grew older, Jem and I thought it generous to allow Atticus thirty minutes to himself [while reading the paper] after supper" (*TKM*, p. 135). Scout surmises, "I sometimes think Atticus subjected every crisis of his life to tranquil evaluation behind *The Mobile Register, The Birmingham News,* and *The Montgomery Advertiser*" (*TKM*, p. 146). Not surprisingly, with a father like Atticus, Scout and Jem turned out to be avid readers themselves. Upon their first encounter, Jem tells Dill that "Scout yonder's been readin' ever since she was born, and she ain't even started school yet" (*TKM*, p. 7). Here is Scout trying to recollect when she first learned how to read:

> I could not remember when the lines above Atticus's moving fingers separated into words, but I had stared at them all the evenings in my memory, listening to the news of the day, Bills to Be Enacted into Laws, the diaries of Lorenzo Dow—anything Atticus happened to be reading when I crawled into his lap every night. Until I feared I would lose it, I never loved to read. One does not love breathing. (*TKM*, p. 18)

When Scout's first-grade teacher instructs her to tell Atticus to stop teaching her how to read, Atticus assuages her fear by striking a compromise:

> "Do you know what a compromise is?" he asked.
> "Bending the law?"
> "No, an agreement reached by mutual concessions. It works this way," he said. "If you'll concede the necessity to go to school, we'll go on reading every night just as we always have. Is it a bargain?"
> "Yes sir!"
> "We'll consider it sealed without the usual formality," Atticus said, when he saw me preparing to spit . .
> Jem and I were accustomed to our father's last-will-and-testament diction, and we were at all times free to interrupt Atticus for a translation when it was beyond our understanding. (*TKM*, p. 31)

In this dialogue, Atticus introduces the word "compromise," which is a moral concept, explains its meaning, and acts on it in a fair transaction between father and daughter, who are accepting the terms as equals.

Atticus instills the ritual of reading in Scout and Jem early in their childhood. "Every night Atticus would read us the sports pages of the newspapers"

(*TKM*, p. 110). Even a boring school curriculum will not discourage the children's love of reading: "No tutorial system devised by man could have stopped him [Jem] from getting at books" (*TKM*, p. 32). The same could be said of Scout. As he begins to experience pubertal changes, Jem goes through a phase where "he didn't want to do anything but read and go off by himself" (*TKM*, p. 138).

It is clear that Atticus is caringly attentive not only to the importance of reading, but also of speaking, of expressing oneself clearly, simply, and eloquently. Written or spoken language is not merely a functional or utilitarian tool for everyday human communication and transaction. Neither is it a means for intellectual understanding alone. Above all, for Harper Lee's Atticus Finch, it is a vehicle for refining and civilizing our human nature. It is a tool for seeking the truth. It is a means for expressing our highest and lowest characteristics, our virtues and vices. It mirrors our essential character. It feeds our imagination, which in turn enriches our capacity for linguistic expression. Atticus's language reflects his truth-seeking intelligence and compassionate heart. It mirrors most if not all of his virtues: his benevolence, charitableness, compassion, courage, decency, determinedness, fairness, generosity, gentleness, humaneness, humility, honesty, innocence, integrity, kindness, objectivity, patience, politeness, pure heartedness, refinement, self-control, selflessness, truthfulness, wisdom, and wholesomeness. Shortly stated, his language reveals his goodness and loving nature. It also discloses his occasional insensitivities, rigidities, and human limitations. In the midst of a sensitive and emotion-filled conversation with his son Jem, Atticus corrects his grammar. To his children he remarks about the wisdom of our foreparents in deciding to exclude women from serving as jurors. He at times gives voice to an "arid" and "impassive self." On one occasion his "curtness" stingingly hurts his daughter's feelings. He also gives way to the human propensity toward, though slight, sadistic humor. He finds amusement in his son's building of a fat snowman who resembles Mr. Avery, a neighbor, and in his daughter's aiming of her air rifle at Miss Maudie's behind. And there comes a time, toward the end of the novel, when Atticus stubbornly and rigidly holds on to the high principle of truthfulness and is momentarily oblivious to the specific human need that the situation calls for: protecting the privacy and fragile integrity of the neighbor, Arthur (Boo) Radley, who has rescued his children by stabbing and killing the evil Bob Ewell. In spite of these and other slippages, Atticus shows the ability to recover his capacity to selflessly take into account the feelings, concerns, and needs of others.

Throughout, in reading *TKM*, the reader gets the sense that in the light of growing up with Atticus's attentive eyes, ears, and voice, Scout and Jem are themselves appropriating highly attuned and sharply differentiating eyes, ears, and voices of their own. Following their father's footsteps, they are becoming good, virtuous individual human beings in their own right. Like her brother Jem, Scout "was more at home in my father's world" (*TKM*, p. 233). They developed a precocious capacity for speaking, reasoning, and appreciating the truth-seeking as well as aesthetic dimensions of language:

"You know, she [Miss Maudie] can talk real pretty sometimes. One time I asked her to have a chew and she said no thanks—chewing gum cleaved to her palate and rendered her speechless," said Jem carefully. "Doesn't that sound nice?"

"Yeah [replied Scout], she can say nice things sometimes." (*TKM*, pp. 61–62)

Atticus's attention to language accords superbly well with Iris Murdoch's understanding of language as, at least potentially, a moral force in our lives. Murdoch would view Atticus's careful, clear, concise, eloquent, responsible, skillful, and other-directed use of language as the embodiment of our highest human perfectibility. When we combine Murdoch's assumption that, in its purest form, language is a moral medium and her assumption that love, in its highest impersonal sense as well as its most intimate sense, is of the essence of morality, then we can derive the logical conclusion that language is the best instrument of our loving orientation toward the world. How we speak and listen to one another mirrors the quality of our loving orientation toward each other.

Language use, however, does not take place in a vacuum. It always occurs in a spatiotemporal context. A word is said to a particular person(s) at a specific time and place. Murdoch includes under context the histories of the speakers and listeners as well as their capacities to imagine the perspective or point of view of one another. Context also includes objects of attention that serve as springboards for dialogue. These objects of attention can be concrete things, images, and ideas or the communicators can serve as each other's objects of attention. Murdoch allows for extraverbal understanding not only to guide our verbal communication but also to unexpectedly emerge from our dialogue when least expected. Moreover, sometimes, we simply cannot say what we see (understand). Sometimes we understand more as we give expression to our thoughts.

Although language can degenerate into degraded forms, it remains our best instrument for becoming good and loving persons. By changing our language, we change how we experience the world. When parents and children become mutual objects of attention and share common objects of attention, they simultaneously come to share a common discourse (language in use). It is not surprising, therefore, to find that in *TKM*, Scout and Jem, having been caringly attended to by and having paid attention to their father over time in their place of dwelling, they begin to echo, in their discourse, his moral voice again and again. Having heard her father say that he tries his best "to love everybody" and it is "not okay to hate anybody," Scout, on overhearing (perceiving) her teacher saying on one occasion that she "hates Hitler a lot" because of his treatment of the Jews, and on another occasion say that "it's time somebody taught 'em [African Americans] a lesson, they were getting' above themselves," tells her brother, "Jem, it's not right to persecute anybody, is it? I mean have mean thoughts about anybody, even, is it?" (*TKM*, p. 247). When toward the end of the novel, her father reaches the agonizing decision to sacrifice his highest principle of truthfulness to protect the privacy and individual fragility of Arthur (Boo) Radley, who has killed the villainous Bob Ewell to save the children and on seeing his dejected deportment, Scout attempts to cheer him up by reassuring him of the rightness of his decision. She explains to him that, "it'd be sort of like shootin' a mockingbird, wouldn't it?" (*TKM*, p. 276). Scout, in this moving moment, is echoing her father's much earlier moral lesson that it is a sin to kill mockingbirds because they do not harm anyone and they only make music and bring pleasure to human beings. Scout, here, is giving voice to the language of love in its highest, simultaneously personal and impersonal, sense.

Atticus's specific attention to language is grounded in his general attentiveness to (deeply felt interest in) the details about his children's lives without becoming intrusive. The narrator, Scout, describes her father in the following terms: "Jem and I found our father satisfactory: he played with us, read to us, and treated us with courteous detachment" (*TKM*, p. 6). "It was our habit to run meet Atticus the moment we saw him round the post office corner in the distance [coming home from his office] . . ; [after my first day at school] he was full of questions about school" (*TKM*, p. 28). Respecting his children's privacy, Atticus would habitually knock at their doors when he wanted to speak with them. As evidence of Atticus's taken-for-granted attentiveness, the narrating Scout says, "As we grew older, Jem and I thought it generous to allow Atticus thirty minutes to himself after supper" (*TKM*, p. 135). After attending Calpurnia's church in her father's absence, which was a new experience for her, Scout adds, "I told him [Atticus] in detail about our trip to church with Calpurnia. Atticus seemed to enjoy it . . " (*TKM*, p. 135). Atticus is not only attentive to his children's needs, but to their emerging capacities and competencies, too. The attentiveness to and the supplying of his children's needs as well as his attunement to and encouragement of their surfacing strengths form the foundation on which a relationship of trust and trustworthiness is built in the context of constant and continuous affection, fairness, flexibility, and firmness. For the most part, Atticus demonstrates repeatedly the ability to move between affectionate and objective attentiveness to each of his children without slipping into suffocating sentimentality or harsh depersonalizing cruelty. This requires the cultivation of the capacity for moral (loving) imagination, the twin partner of attention.

2. Imagination

There is a moral lesson in which Atticus Finch tries to teach his children that gets to the heart of the meaning of Harper Lee's story. The lesson is simply this: [Here Atticus is instructing his daughter, Scout, on how to "get along with all kinds of folks"] "You never really understand a person until you consider things from his point of view" (*TKM*, p. 30). This ability to perceive other individuals from their point of view is essentially, but not exclusively, what Iris Murdoch means by (moral) imagination. When her brother Jem is "moody and silent for a week,"

Scout remembers her father's teaching: "As Atticus once advised me to do, I tried to climb into Jem's skin and walk around in it" (*TKM,* p. 57). More importantly, Atticus encourages his children to take the point of view of those who are quite other than themselves; those who are seemingly very different, strange, or even bad. He urges them to picture themselves in the place of two figures who show intent to harm him, Walter Cunningham and Robert Ewell, because he aims to or has defended Tom Robinson:

> Mr. Cunningham's basically a good man . . he just has his blind spots along with the rest of us. . . . A mob's always made up of people, no matter what. Mr. Cunningham was part of a mob last night, but he was still a man. . . So it took an eight-year-old child to bring 'em to their senses, didn't it? . . That proves something—that a gang of wild animals *can* be stopped, simply because they're still human . . you children last night made Walter Cunningham stand in my shoes for a minute. That was enough. . . . I don't want either of you bearing a grudge about this, no matter what happens. (*TKM,* pp. 157–58)

And again,

> Jem, see if you can stand in Bob Ewell's shoes a minute. I destroyed his last shred of credibility at that trial, if he had any to begin with. The man had to have some kind of comeback, his kind always does. So if spitting in my face and threatening me saved Mayella Ewell [Bob Ewell's daughter] one extra beating, that's something I'll gladly take. He had to take it out on somebody and I'd rather it be me than that houseful of children out there. You understand? (*TKM,* P. 218)

Moreover, throughout the novel, Scout and Jem, along with their friend Dill, struggle to understand what it is like to be the reclusive, never seen until nearing the end, neighbor, Boo Radley. They exercise their imagination, through dramatic play, in order to fathom this unfathomable other. They are at the same time attempting to tame their fears of this unknown and unknowable different "other" through playful but at the same time serious enactments of a continually created and recreated imaginative narrative based on few facts, observations, and many rumors and hearsay. For Murdoch, metaphors, parables, and dramatic stories and plays have the potential to accentuate our imaginative capacity to understand dissimilar others. Together with these dramatic enactments of the life of Boo Radley, Scout and Jem repeatedly make an effort to imaginatively comprehend Boo's oblique display of selfless acts of generosity and love directed toward them (leaving small presents for them in a hole in a tree; mending Jem's torn pants, left behind while escaping the Radley property; putting a blanket on the shivering Scout, while watching men put out the fire at Miss Maudie's house). Scout finally encounters Boo Radley in her own home after he saves her and her brother's lives by killing Bob Ewell, toward the end of the novel. It is at this point that she comes truly to perceive (understand) the beauty and goodness of this particular and unique other. She reflects: "Atticus was right. One time he said you never really know a man until you stand in his shoes and walk around in them. Just standing on the Radley porch [having walked Boo home] was enough" (*TKM,* p. 279). Through her creative, imaginative effort, Scout is finally able to transcend the dichotomous and disjunctive images of Boo Radley in her mind, the bad Boo versus the good Boo, and comes to see him for what he is: Like a mockingbird, he was put here on earth to bring music (delight) to his (symbolic) children's lives. And when "Boo's children needed him," he is there to protect them.

In our interpersonal world, our imaginative mental activity is an essential medium for connecting or joining us to others. Our capacity for imagination is inexhaustible. At the same time, the reality of others is also inexhaustible. Our imagination makes it possible for us to view others from multiple points of view or perspectives. As a result, we can understand them better. Our imaginative faculty enables us to visualize what is valuable or desirable in the long run and prepares us for action. We can imagine the needs of essential others and initiate the process of supplying them. Imagination empowers us to foresee the consequences of our actions such as the impact they will have on or the different interpretations they will trigger from others.

As a father, Atticus demonstrates his immense capacity for (empathic) imagination. To illustrate, here is a conversation taking place between Atticus and his brother, Jack, who has been told shortly before that he "didn't understand children much and . . why" by Scout, his niece (the reconciliatory interaction between Scout and her Uncle Jack has followed an episode in which Scout has used bad language, had engaged in a fist fight with her cousin Francis who had called her father a "nigger lover," and had been physically punished by Uncle Jack for her verbal and physical behavior, without taking into account her side of the story):

> [Uncle Jack is addressing Atticus; meanwhile, Scout is listening in on the conversation, while Atticus is aware she is listening and wants her "to hear every word he said."] "Her use of bathroom invective leaves nothing to the imagination. But she doesn't know the meaning of half she says—she asked me what a whore-lady was . . "
> "Did you tell her?"
> "No, I told her about Lord Melbourne."
> "Jack, when a child asks you something, answer him, for goodness' sake. But don't make a production of it. Children are children, but they can spot an evasion quicker than adults, and evasion simply muddles 'em. No . . . you had the right answer this afternoon, but the wrong reasons. Bad language is a stage all children go through, and it dies with time when they learn they're not attracting attention with it. Hotheadedness isn't. Scout's got to learn to

keep her head and learn soon, with what's in store for her these next few months. She's coming along, though. Jem's getting older and she follows his example a good bit now. All she needs is assistance sometimes."
"Atticus, you've never laid a hand on her."
"I admit that. So far I've been able to get by with threats. Jack, she minds me as well as she can. Doesn't come up to scratch half the time, but she tries."
"That's not the answer. . . ."
"No, the answer is she knows I know she tries. That's what makes the difference." (*TKM,* pp. 87–88)

Through his imaginative effort and wisdom, Atticus shows his understanding of children in general and his daughter in particular. When children ask questions, they want straightforward and truthful answers they can comprehend. Children go through a stage of development where they use bad language to attract the attention of and have an impact on the important adults in their world. Children have the natural tendency to model themselves after parents and their older siblings. Atticus envisions that following Jem's example will have a good effect on Scout. Atticus is also able to project himself into the inner life of his daughter and affirm the fact that she does try to live by his guidance and that she knows that her father knows she tries. "That's what makes the difference."

Throughout the novel, Atticus shows his empathic attunement to his children's affective states. He is physically affectionate, especially toward Scout. (Here Atticus's limited vision of masculinity is a by-product of his time and place.) Atticus's welcoming lap is always ready to receive Scout and provide her with soothing comfort, especially in times of turmoil. At such times, he is there for his children when they need him, calming them with words and physical gestures of tender, loving care. One of the repeated calming and reassuring phrases that he directs to his children when they are experiencing anxiety, fear, concern, or stress is "It's not time to worry." Interestingly, Jem emulates his father by using this phrase in many instances that required comforting his sister. Scout uses this phrase to reduce her own concern over her brother by addressing it to herself. They both appropriate the capacity for empathic attunement from their father. "Jem was becoming almost as good as Atticus at making you feel right when things went wrong" (*TKM,* p. 259). Toward that touching conclusion, when Atticus suffers the agony of deciding between principle (truthfulness) and individual reality and need (the welfare of Boo Radley) and choosing in favor of the latter, it is Scout who gives comfort to Atticus:

Atticus sat looking at the floor for a long time. I ran to him and hugged him and kissed him with all my might. "Yes sir, I understand," I reassured him. "Mr. Tate [the Sheriff of Maycomb who had already decided and was trying to persuade the reluctant Atticus] was right."
Atticus disengaged himself and looked at me. "What do you mean?"

"Well, it'd be sort of like shootin' a mockingbird, wouldn't it?"
Atticus put his face in my hair and rubbed it. When he got up and walked
across the porch into the shadows, his youthful step had returned. (*TKM*, p.
276)

Murdoch has more in mind regarding the meaning of imagination. For her,
imagination is an active, constructive process of reasoning. It is an operation of the
mind that searches for and seeks coherence. At its best, it is a truth-seeking creative
intelligence. It is an inner activity of the senses that is capable of perceiving
difference in sameness and sameness in difference. A fly and a tree are different,
but they are the same in that they are both living organisms. To imagine is to form
and re-form schemes or categories of objects, persons, or events. It is to play with
possibilities and patterns, with kinesthetic (bodily) sensations, images, and (abstract) ideas. It is to anticipate the ripple effects of one's contemplated actions.
Imagination involves the ability to see relationships between parts and wholes,
parts and parts, and wholes and larger wholes in our perceptual world. It consists
of the capacity to perceive the interconnection between figure and ground, between the object of attention and its multiple spatiotemporal contexts. To be
engaged in proper imaginative activity is to become forgetful of the self. It is an
honest, free, and truth-seeking effort. To be engaged in improper imaginative
activity (what Murdoch calls fantasy) is to be self-absorbed and preoccupied. It is
to be driven by self-centered sensations, images, and thoughts (aims, goals, and
preferences). Improper imagination is propelled by narcissistic needs and desires.
It is fuelled by unrealistic and untruthful pictures of self, others, and world. It is
energized by false ideas and ideals. Improper imaginative activity aims at magically
bending reality to suit one's selfish and deluded willfulness. It serves the purpose of
seeking self-inflation (power) or avoiding self-deflation (powerlessness). It protects
the self from pain and consoles the self with the fleeting feeling of self-importance.
Whereas improper imagination imprisons the soul and clouds its moral vision,
proper imagination frees the soul and clears its moral vision. Whereas improper
imagination falls for momentary shifts in emotions and motivations, proper imagination brackets and keeps a lead on such fluctuations. Whereas improper imagination is grounded in falsification and irrationality, proper imagination is rooted
in reason and selfless (rational) emotions. Lastly, whereas improper imagination
leads to compulsive, self-seeking, and bad conduct, proper imagination results in
creative, other-directed, and good conduct. In everyday life, there is a graduated
range between the degree with which we make or fail to make use of our capacity
for proper imagination. Proper love requires the constant purification of our
imagination.

As a parent, citizen-lawyer, and a human being, Atticus Finch is a man of
moral imagination. His reasonable foresightedness, which unfolds naturally and
spontaneously, typifies the stylistic manner with which he reacts to particular
realities of everyday life, at home or in public. In his mind's eye, he has an

unwavering picture of the guises of goodness: innocence, perfection (or perfect-ibility), purity, and simplicity, and of the path that leads toward the good: love, with all its ingredients (attention, imagination, [compassionate] detachment, hu-mility, truthfulness [honesty], courage, and justice [fairness]). For Harper Lee's Atticus, children embody this picture of goodness. However, they need the con-stant loving guidance and nurturance of adults to keep this capacity for goodness alive. They need to be taught by way of words and example. At the same time, children need to be monitored and discouraged from pursuing their fantasy-based egocentric tendencies. This is the optimal aim of parenting: to picture (imagine) the good and to become good. Not to be guided by self-seeking fantasy (improper imagination) constitutes the other side of the same coin. Atticus struggles not to succumb to the temptation of power seeking and neither does he encourage the enactment of such fantasies in his children. He refuses to rely on the power of the gun, in spite of his excellent marksmanship, even in self-defense. He instructs his children not to fight back, similarly, not even for self-defense. He exhorts them to hold their head high and be gentle-persons. He is placing before them a meta-phorical moral picture of the kind of persons they need to become. Upon seeing his father display his talent as a sharp shooter and refuse to take false pride (a form of fantasy-based self-inflation) in his giftedness, Jem suddenly is insightful about the meaning of his father's refusal. He tells his sister, "If he was proud of it, he'da told us . . [but] Atticus is a gentleman, just like me!" (*TKM*, pp. 98–99). And when a classmate in school, Cecil Jacobs, calls Atticus a "disgrace" for defending Tom Robinson, Scout says,

> I drew a bead on him, remembered what Atticus had said, then dropped my fists and walked away, "Scout's a coward!" ringing in my ears. It was the first time I ever walked away from a fight.
>
> Somehow, if I fought Cecil I would let Atticus down. Atticus so rarely asked Jem and me to do something for him, I could take being called a coward for him. I felt extremely *noble* for having remembered, and re-mained noble for three weeks. (*TKM*, pp. 76–77; emphasis added)

For Atticus, the picture (image) of a good person calls on him to conduct himself truthfully and nonduplicitously. This is how he sees himself. This is how he wants to be seen by others, especially his children. He tells his children that if he does not conduct himself as an upholder and defender of the truth, he will lose his moral authority. He will no longer be able to face them and look them in the eye. He will have lost them. Before Scout and Jem look at anyone else they look at him. He has tried to live so that he can look squarely back at them. "I don't want to lose him [Jem] and Scout, because they're all I've got" (*TKM*, p. 273). Through the media-tion of essential others in our, especially early, lives, we imagine the kind of persons we can become and then to live in the light of that imagination. Atticus succeeds not only in modeling, instilling, and nurturing in his children a picture of goodness, which they strive to approximate, but also in creating a home atmosphere where their imaginative reasoning flourishes.

3. Compassionate Detachment

This is an inherent ingredient of love. To love others is to perceive them as individuals who are similar to and different from ourselves, with needs and desires of their own. This kind of perception requires a certain degree of detachment. Detachment is the unsentimental contemplation of objects, persons, or events. However, it is not to be confused with a state of indifference or passivity. It is a kind of sympathetic objectivity. To perceive things or persons with detachment is to look at them with compassion. Detachment turns out, paradoxically, to be grounded in the most unselfish, unpossessive form of human attachment. It is not the grasping, sentimental, or fantasy-based type of attachment. To view others with compassionate detachment means seeing oneself in others. It is to view others with kindness and felt connectedness. In a state of sympathetic detachment, the self (ego) is either absent or minimally present. To be concernedly detached is to be disengaged from our own personal prejudices. Selfless detachment enables us to know others objectively and realistically. It protects us from succumbing to the natural tendency to see others as belonging to our fantasy world. Compassionate detachment can also be directed toward ourselves. From this detached perspective, we can learn to view ourselves objectively. To exemplify this point, Murdoch mentions something that the poet Rainer Maria Rilke learned from a friend while looking at some pictures by Paul Cezanne. This learning, which leaves a lasting impact upon Rilke, has to do with Cezanne's ability to paint his self-portraits from a detached viewpoint. His detachment is compared to that of a dog viewing himself in the mirror and seeing (and painting!) just another dog, without the distortions of an anxious and biased self. To be detached, however, does not mean that one is disengaged from the object of attention. The object of perception is now perceived from a different and more penetrating perspective. A truer and more real self is unveiled to the detached Cezanne. This is exactly what fascinates the viewer of Cezanne's self-portraits. What Murdoch says of goodness can be said of detachment. According to Murdoch, one can be "good" in one domain and "bad" in other domains of one's life. Cezanne can be "good" in his artwork, but not as a husband or a father. Murdoch still allows for the possible spread effect of goodness from one area to other areas, even though it may be slight. Similarly, one can display the capacity for distancing in one domain, but not others. The spread effect, when significant, contributes to the wholeness and integrity of the individual. Moreover, character strengths such as patience, perdurance, perseverance, self-control (resistance to impulsivity, temptations, and imperial self-assertion), and tolerance are all capacities of detachment or psychological (psychosocial) distancing.

Atticus Finch is a superb practitioner of the artful discipline of compassionate detachment. At the beginning of *TKM*, he is described by Scout as a father who "treated us with courteous detachment" (*TKM*, p. 6). But it is a "courteous detachment" anchored in passionate attachment. There is no question in the mind of the reader of *TKM* that Atticus is kind, caring, and compassionate, not only toward his children but toward everyone. He tries his "best to love everybody" (*TKM*, p. 108). He feels a deep abiding connection (attachment) toward his fellow human beings. This felt connectedness is not based on superficial sentimentality or idealistic illusion. He lives his compassion with a sense of detached practicality. It is a kind of pragmatic humanitarianism. He does not seek to control (have power over) or compare himself to others. Comparison and control are incompatible with compassion. He maintains his compassionate disposition toward his fellow human beings even in the most trying of circumstances. In the trial of Tom Robinson, Atticus asks Mayella Ewell, while cross-examining her,

> "Do you want to tell us what happened?"
> But she did not hear the compassion in his invitation. . . Somehow Atticus had hit her hard in a way that was not clear to me, but it gave him no pleasure to do so. (*TKM*, p. 188)

With the exception of his final appeal to the jury, his courtroom voice is described as having a "detached" quality. This professional voice is further depicted as arid. It is even used outside the courtroom, when Atticus needs to be firm with his children: "It took Atticus's courtroom voice to drag us away from the tree" (*TKM*, p. 90). Nevertheless, from the reader's perspective, Atticus's everyday voice can be described as clear, controlled, low keyed, and measured; yet, simultaneously, it is spontaneous, sincere, and resonant. The narrator, Scout, says, "I never heard Atticus raise his voice in my life, except to a deaf witness" (*TKM*, p. 172). In another reference, she recalls, "the only time I ever heard Atticus speak sharply to anyone was when I once heard him say, 'Sister, I do the best I can with them!' It had to do with my going around in overalls" (*TKM*, p. 81). On rare occasions, Atticus uncharacteristically labels those people who take advantage of or violate the rights of vulnerable others (such as whites cheating blacks) as "trash." Similarly, children, too, are vulnerable to the manipulations and mistreatments of adults.

Atticus's voice bodies forth the detached compassion of his loving character. All the capacities of compassionate detachment (patience, endurance, perseverance, self-control, and tolerance) typify his mode of being and behaving in the everyday world of Maycomb. Scout comments, "I sometimes think Atticus subjected every crisis in his life to tranquil evaluation behind *The Mobile Register, The Birmingham News,* and *The Montgomery Advertiser*" (*TKM*, p. 146). And again, Atticus has an "infinite capacity for calming turbulent seas" (*TKM*, p. 169).

Interestingly, the narrator mentions a couple of ritualistic habits that Atticus has acquired that help him distance himself and gain perspective on a tension-laden situation. In such circumstances, either "His fingers wandered to his watchpocket; he said that was the only way he could think" (*TKM*, p. 29; see also p. 222) or "Atticus put his foot on the rung of a chair and rubbed his hand slowly down the side of his thigh" (*TKM*, p. 95; see also p. 210). Manners, for Atticus, are a means of maintaining his compassionate distance. Manners are not merely a veneer of civility that serve the purpose of lubricating the machinery of everyday social functioning. Good manners are essential to the maintenance of goodness. Atticus is courteous inside and outside his home. During the trial, Judge Taylor informs Mayella Ewell that "Mr. Finch is always courteous to everybody" (*TKM*, p. 182). In comparing two good characters in the novel, the narrator Scout ruminates, "It occurred to me that in their own way, Tom Robinson's manners were as good as Atticus's" (*TKM*, p. 195). Atticus urges and encourages his children to appropriate good manners and to pause and think before they speak and act out. "Be a gentleman [or a lady]," "Hold your head high," and "Keep your head" are verbal instructions that Atticus repeatedly gives to his children. Scout and Jem gradually internalize these guides to self-conduct. The chapter on or the episode involving Mrs. Henry Lafayette Dubose in *TKM* demonstrates nicely how Jem comes to learn the lesson of being a gentleman and keeping his head at the same time. Mrs. Dubose, a neighbor, is a cantankerous, sickly, old lady who is addicted to morphine as a painkiller and is resolved to rid herself of this chemical dependency before she dies. She verbally torments the children, every time they pass her house, about their manners, morals, and their father's doings.

> Countless evenings Atticus would find Jem furious at something Mrs. Dubose had said when we went by.
>
> "Easy does it, son," Atticus would say. "She's an old lady and she's ill. You just hold your head high and be a gentleman. Whatever she says to you, it's your job not to let her make you mad."
>
> Jem would say that she must not be very sick, she hollered so. When the three of us came to her house, Atticus would sweep off his hat, wave gallantly to her and say, "Good evening, Mrs. Dubose! You look like a picture this evening."
>
> I never heard Atticus say like a picture of what. He would tell her the courthouse news, and would say he hoped with all his heart she'd have a good day tomorrow. He would return his hat to his head, swing me on his shoulders in her very presence, and we would go home in the twilight. It was times like these when I thought my father, who hated guns and had never been to any wars, was the bravest man who ever lived. (*TKM*, p. 100)

Having just turned twelve and while undergoing a "phase of self-conscious rectitude," Jem, upon being subjected along with his sister to the unrelenting verbal harassments of Mrs. Dubose, would instruct Scout, "Don't pay attention to her, just hold your head high and be a gentleman[!]" (*TKM,* p. 101). One day, however, Jem loses his head and decapitates Mrs. Dubose's camellias, while she is not watching. As a form of punishment for his misbehavior, Mrs. Dubose demands that Jem read to her every afternoon and Saturdays for a month. Atticus agrees, sensing immediately that this is an opportunity for Jem to learn about compassionate detachment and courage (the courage of Mrs. Dubose in conquering her addiction). "Through the weeks he [Jem] had cultivated an expression of *polite* and *detached* interest, which he would present to her in answer to her most blood-curdling inventions" (*TKM,* p. 110; emphasis added). Guided by his compassionate detachment, Atticus's good intentions are realized. But, as Murdoch recognizes, compassionate detachment does not guarantee rational results or good endings. Atticus's sympathetic objectivity does not protect him against the evil intentions and actions of Bob Ewell. Only the providential intervention of Boo Radley saves the children from Ewell's murderous attempt on their lives. In the presence of such miraculous mediation Atticus is resignedly grateful. In a moving moment, just before Boo is led to his own house by Scout, Atticus says to him, "Thank you for my children, Arthur" (*TKM,* p. 276).

4. Humility

In the eyes of Iris Murdoch, if there is one character trait that captures the heart of goodness of selflessly loving individuals, it is humility. Good people are humble people. Humble persons are selflessly respectful of reality. They recognize and respect the independent reality of others. They have a detached perspective on their own reality. They realize that their own and others' perspective on reality is partial and limited; that their capacity and those of others for meaning-making is also limited. This realization predisposes them to remain open and invite the perspective of others who are different from themselves. Humble individuals have a realistic perspective on their own strengths and weaknesses. They do not overestimate or underestimate their abilities and limitations. Thus, they try to make the best they can with the qualities they have. Humble persons are realistic about their slight or lack of control over events outside of themselves. They are aware of their limitations in the face of the contingencies of existence, such as accidents, chance, death, or other unpredictable life events. Contingencies also include their own limitedness and fallibility. Their acceptance of these contingencies, however, does not prevent them from their responsible pursuit of goodness. Humble people have a realistic picture of their insignificance in the larger scheme of the universe. They are aware of their existence as small vanishing points on the spatiotemporal graph of history. On the one hand, they are cognizant of the pointlessness of existence; on the other hand, they are mindful of its all-important value in its endless call to virtuous action.

When an attempt is made to find key descriptive terms and phrases that make up the personality profile or the character portrait of humble persons, it becomes clear why Murdoch is of the conviction that humility comes close to capturing love's essential virtues (see Table 1). And Atticus Finch is the perfect exemplar of the humble person. In fact, Harper Lee describes her beloved father, who serves as her real-life model for her fictional hero, as a person whose humility lends him a sense of dignity.

Humility shines through the demeanor and mannerisms of Atticus Finch throughout the dramatic unfolding of the narrative of *TKM*. He lives out his humility in private and in public. In his home, with his children, he is able to achieve a sensitive balance between being humble and being firm and fair; between humility and the assertion of authority; between respectfully relating to them on an egalitarian basis as two unique, autonomous individuals and relating to them in his role as the final voice of authority, as evaluator, judge, and arbitrator. He shows respect for their privacy by not intruding into their free physical and psychological space that he has created for them, but only up to a certain point and within a delimited range. When he senses that the children are rehearsing, planning, and acting upon a script which calls for violating the privacy of their neighbor, Boo Radley, he intervenes to forbid them from playing "an asinine game he had seen us playing or making fun of anybody on this street or in this town" or "putting his [Mr. Radley's] life's history on display for the edification of the neighborhood"; "How would we like it if Atticus barged in on us without knocking, when we were in our rooms at night?" (*TKM*, p. 49). As a loving father, Atticus always seeks his children's good, but never at the expense of seeking the common communal good. Being sharply attuned to their level of maturity, Atticus extends to Scout and Jem a delimited range of freedoms and entitlements. At the same time he has realistic expectations regarding the assumption of responsible conduct on their part, knowing fully well that some of it takes time, guidance, and encouragement to achieve. He makes challenging but never excessive demands of them. They sense this and do not want to disappoint him. They desire to live up to his realistic expectations.

Atticus's parenting style is democratic and nonauthoritarian. To begin with, he allows his children to call him by his first name. Yet, they never interpret this as a leeway for permissiveness. They are always respectful, natural, and spontaneous in the manner they address and speak to their father. They sometimes call him Sir. He in turn speaks to them as adults. He never talks down to them. He never seeks to dominate or control (exercise power over) them. For the most part, he is noncoercive in his disciplining style. Although he uses mild but firm verbal threats, always coupled with explanations, he never uses physical punishment. Reflecting on this, Jem says to his sister, "It's like this, Scout . . Atticus ain't ever whipped me since I can remember. I wanta keep it that way" (*TKM*, p. 56). In his interactions with them, he never raises his voice. He does not displace his frustrations upon them. He does not use them as a means for his own ends. He brackets

TABLE 1
Attributes of Persons of Humility

Accepting	Loyal
Benevolent	Merciful/Pitying
Calm/composed	Obedient (to the authority of goodness)
Caring	Open (to change)
Cheerful/Good-spirited	Other centered
Civil/humane	Passionate
Conscientious	Patient
Consistent/Constant	Peace loving
Courageous	Persistent/Persevering
Decisive/Resolute	Playful
Devoted (to person or project beyond self)	Power/Control avoiding
	Practical
Dignified	Pure hearted
Disciplined	Quietness valuing
Dutiful	Rational/Reasonable (person with good judgment)
Effort generating/Initiative taking	
Egalitarian	Realistic
Eloquent/Clear	Refined
Empathic	Reliable
Faith-ful (full of faith in goodness)	Respectful
Forgiving	Self-aware/Self-knowledgeable
Generous	Self-controlled (person of controlled passion)
Gentle	
Good willed	Service oriented
Grateful	Simple
Hopeful	Steadfast
Humorous (not overly serious)	Sympathetic (concern for others)
Independent (yet interdependent)	Temperate
Innocent	Tolerant
Inspired (by perfection/excellence)	Trusting/Trustworthy
Integrated (person of integrity)	Truthful (truth and knowledge seeking)/Honest
Intelligent (emotionally)	
Invisibility preferring	Unpretentious
Just/Fair	Unselfish (Selfless/Self-sacrificing)
Kind	Wise

his own self-interests and needs in order to be attuned to their interests and needs, which he attempts to meet to the best of his ability and to the degree of their appropriateness. He brings to their attention objects, events, and notions he believes will contribute to their maturation and good. He tries to cultivate in them a selfless interest in things, persons, and events outside of themselves. For example, "Atticus had said [to his children] it was the polite thing to talk to people about what they were interested in, not about what you were interested in" (*TKM*, p. 154). He is at the same time affirmingly and encouragingly attuned to their own evolving interests and unfolding talents. When Jem creates a caricature of Mr. Avery, their neighbor, in the form of a snowman, Atticus responds,

> Son, I can't tell you what you're going to be—an engineer, a lawyer, or a portrait painter . . but from now on I'll never worry about what'll become of you son, you'll always have an idea. . . You've perpetrated a near libel here in the front yard. We've got to disguise this fellow [for he approximates too close a facsimile of the real-life neighbor, Mr. Avery]. (*TKM*, p. 67)

Atticus praises his son's artistic aptitude, expresses his own delight, points to openended vocational ramifications, and asks Jem to disguise his creation in order not to hurt the feelings or make a fool of Mr. Avery. All in all, Atticus allows his children the freedom to be and become themselves.

Of the attributes mentioned in Table 1, there are six characteristics of loving humility (unselfishness, justice, truthfulness, cheerfulness, courage, and wisdom) which require special elaboration because they simultaneously elucidate the essential structure of love.

5. Unselfishness (Selflessness)

There is no question that Atticus Finch is an unselfish man. He selflessly recognizes and respects the similar and different realities of other fellow human beings. This is what he is to make of his life: to selflessly serve others to the best of his ability and in response to the call of his conscience. He aims at promoting the welfare and growth of others. His children are very special "others." He unselfconsciously immerses himself in familial and communal concentric circles of care, concern, devotion, and loyalty in the pursuit of his moral life project of selflessly serving others.

Selflessness does not mean the disappearance or the destruction of the self. It simply means that the self is placed in proper (modest) perspective, relative to one's place in the world (universe). Unselfishness or selflessness refers to the absence of selfishness or self-inflation. To be selflessly oriented is to be other-centered rather than self-centered. The "other" can be a person, object, or project. Paradoxically, being oriented toward and taking care of the other contributes to one's growth and well-being although that is not consciously aimed for or guaranteed.

Atticus's children observe their father display unselfish conduct in his everyday life inside and outside the home. He is selflessly there for them at home. He is selflessly there for others. Being there for them is taken for granted by the children when they are young. As Jem approaches adolescence, he begins to realize that his father has worries, whereas Scout does not realize this yet: "He [Atticus]'s got a lot on his mind now, without us worrying him." "Like what? [Scout replies] Atticus didn't appear to have anything on his mind." "It's this Tom Robinson case that's worrying him to death" (*TKM*, pp. 137–38). Atticus's calm, composed, and compassionate orientation toward his children never fluctuates in the midst of this worrying. Above all, he is worried about the deleterious effect of the case on the children and not himself.

There are many other observations of Atticus's selfless interest in others. "During his first five years in Maycomb, Atticus practiced economy more than anything; for several years thereafter he invested his earnings in his brother's education" (*TKM*, p. 5). A poor farmer-client consults Atticus in his home. Before he leaves, the children hear him say, "Mr. Finch, I don't know when I'll ever be able to repay you." " 'Let that be the least of your worries, Walter,' Atticus said" (*TKM*, p. 20). While Scout listens, Miss Maudie describes Atticus as one of a handful of people in Maycomb who have "enough *humility* to think, when they look at a Negro, there but for the Lord's kindness am I" (*TKM*, p. 236; emphasis added). On a separate occasion she says to Scout and Jem, "I simply want to tell you that there are some men in this world who were born to do our unpleasant jobs for us. Your father's one of them" (*TKM*, p. 215). Interestingly, the nickname Scout itself denotes selfless service to others. And the name Jem (Jeremy) has the spiritual connotation of humility.

Over time, the children come to the realization that their father is not the kind of person who will inflate himself through taking false pride in his accomplishments, talents, education, intelligence, and family background. They learn that is in part what it means to be a gentle person. Atticus tells Scout "one time that most of this Old Family's stuff's foolishness because everybody's just as old as everybody else's" (*TKM*, p. 226). Scout absorbs the lesson when she in turn tells Jem, "I think there's just one kind of folks. Folks" (*TKM*, p. 227). But the ultimate test of selfless humility is shown in how Atticus conducts himself when he is subjected to (physical) humiliation. Miss Stephanie Crawford, another neighbor, tells Scout and Jem:

> [T]his morning Mr. Bob Ewell stopped Atticus on the post office corner, spat in his face, and told him he'd get him if it took the rest of his life. . . . Atticus didn't bat an eye, just took out his handkerchief and wiped his face and stood there and let Mr. Ewell call him names wild horses could not bring her to repeat. Mr. Ewell was a veteran of an obscure war; that plus

Atticus's peaceful reaction probably prompted him to inquire, "Too proud to fight, you nigger-lovin' bastard?" . . Atticus said, "No, too old," put his hands in his pockets and strolled on. . . [Y]ou had to hand it to Atticus Finch, he could be right dry sometimes. . . "I wish Bob Ewell wouldn't chew tobacco," was all Atticus said about it. (*TKM*, p. 217)

In explaining this episode to his children, Atticus reminds them of the principle of imaginative and detached compassion: to put themselves in Bob Ewell's shoes and walk in them. The point to be made here is that the less we are invested in ourselves (the more selfless we are) the less vulnerable we are to the slights and woundings of others. The more humble we are, the less the effect of everyday humiliations that are directed toward us. Conversely, the more egoistic we are, the more we use up our energies to defend and shore up our fragile egos. We make use of this bad but powerful energy system to shore up the self, in comparison to others, by being possessive and controlling of our children; by living vicariously through our children, by not allowing our children to be and become themselves. The same energy system is applied to objects and people other than our children. The less we are invested in ourselves, the more (good) energy we have at our disposal to enable us to focus on and satisfy the needs of our children and persons beyond our family circle.

6. Justice (Fairness)

For Murdoch, to be loving (attentive, imaginative, compassionately detached, and humble) is to be just. The loving gaze (of parents) is a just gaze. When we are selflessly respectful of the reality of others, we are optimally positioned to treat them fairly. There is, therefore, a positive correlation between unselfishness and fairness and a negative correlation between selfishness and fairness. Selfless parents are fair parents; narcissistic parents are likely to be unfair toward their children. Children show a natural and gradual intuitive grasp of fairness. The maturation of this understanding and its application in everyday life requires learning through explanation, encouragement, and example.

There is no doubt in the minds of Scout and Jem that their loving father is a fair man. His verbal threats and nonphysical punishments are proper and equitable. He does not use them unless he has to and, when he does, they are utilized with their welfare in mind. Because his ego is not on the line, his disciplining style is used as a vehicle for their edification. For example, he sends his son to read to Mrs. Dubose not only to rectify his misbehavior but, more importantly, to learn something about compassionate detachment and the physical courage of Mrs. Dubose. Because his ego is out of gear, he is able to know when his children are trying, and they know that he knows they are trying, to live up to his expectations. This enables him to be more tolerant and less hard on them. Moreover, he does not place unnecessary and excessive demands on them. His expectations are, nevertheless, high and at the same time realizable. Sensing his fairness and devotion to their welfare only increases their motivation to live up to his expectations.

In his role as a mediator in his children's conflicts, Atticus is evenhanded. He listens to both sides before rendering a judgment. When appropriate, he urges them to settle their conflicts on their own and by themselves. He also asks them to respectfully "mind" the other adult figures in their home: Calpurnia and, later, Aunt Alexandra. He further instills in them the spirit of compromise and cooperation, naturally, not always successfully. When Scout and Jem react with feelings of hurt, anger, wounded pride, and a readiness for revengeful retaliation to being unfairly and cruelly treated by relatives, schoolmates, neighbors, and townspeople, he encourages prudence, empathic understanding, forbearance, and forgiveness. As a just parent, Atticus is succeeding in raising his children who are precocious perceivers of acts of justice and injustice; children who are being prepared to conduct themselves justly even in the face of an unjust world.

7. Truthfulness (Honesty)

Loving humility requires a truth-seeking and a truth-abiding intelligence which is exercised in daily living. It is lived, however, with the awareness that one's hold on truth is fragile, limited, and partial. It is pursued and practiced with an open mind and a mindful heart. Ultimate truths have to do with seeking answers to questions regarding goodness: how to be and become a good person. From a Murdochian viewpoint, this is the most important truth we seek, and at the same time, this truth seeking will be experienced at times as completely worthless and pointless. We are thrown into this moral world without our say, yet to be moral (good) is our most important choice. Truth seeking aims at synthesizing the contradictions that we are. Truth seeking and truth abiding require selflessness, attentiveness, imagination, and detached compassion. The virtues of the loving orientation always call on one another. More specifically, truthfulness calls on us to be truthful with ourselves and with others, while at the same time taking into account the context in which we find ourselves. Truthfulness demands of us that we trust and become trustworthy in the eyes of others. Again, contextual appropriateness is relevant to the issue of trust. Lastly, truthfulness requires clarity of thought and controlled passion, a kind of balance between our rational and emotional ways of being and acting in the world.

Atticus has devoted his life to seeking and abiding by the truth. He cares about the truth. Truthfulness is manifested in the way he speaks, reasons, and conducts himself. He is a man of integrity. His inquiries are guided by his concern for the truth. He is a clear thinker, a cogent arguer, and a methodical presenter of factual evidence. His genuineness shines through his emotional, attitudinal, and behavioral expressions. He is a man who acts on his truth-based convictions, which will not fluctuate because of outside pressures. He exercises his truth-based judgments in deciding which aspects of his surrounding conventional traditions to accept and which ones to reject. He resists any form of self-deception, which may serve the purpose of minimizing his pains and maximizing his pleasures, in order to live up to his moral responsibilities. He embodies Murdoch's metaphorical equation which discloses the fundamental truth: Truth=Love=Goodness=Reality. Our ultimate reality is goodness, which is revealed through our loving orientation. Atticus's life and work embody this fundamental truth. The reality of others becomes known to us through our loving disposition. At the conclusion of *TKM*, Atticus says to his daughter, "Most people are ["real nice" or good], Scout, when you finally see [lovingly understand] them" (*TKM*, p. 281).

In his communication with his children, Atticus is always truthful. He admonishes his brother for not being straightforward with Scout. Scout and Jem rely on their father's truthfulness. Just like the air they breathe, they take it for granted. Scout tells her friend Dill, "When he [Atticus] wants you to know somethin', he tells you" (*TKM*, p. 141). From her father, Scout has learned the rightness of genuineness and the wrongness of duplicity. What is awe inspiring about Scout's character is her authenticity and spontaneous simplicity. She tells Mr. Raymond, a Maycombian landowner with background, who cohabits with a Negro woman with whom he has fathered mixed children, and who pretends to be a drunkard in order to give the townspeople an excuse for his eccentric conduct, "That ain't honest, Mr. Raymond, making yourself out badder'n you are already" (*TKM*, p. 200). When Scout and Jem begin to be subjected to verbal attacks on their father, Atticus says to his brother, knowing that Scout is upstairs listening, "I just hope that Jem and Scout come to me for their answers instead of listening to the town. I hope they trust me enough" (*TKM*, p. 88). When Atticus is agonizingly torn between disclosing the truth about who killed Bob Ewell and protecting the fragile privacy of Boo Radley, he voices the concern that if he colludes in perpetuating an untruthful explanation for Ewell's murder he will lose the trust of his children and compromise his own integrity and uprightness. He says to Mr. Tate, the sheriff of Maycomb County, "If they [his children] don't trust me they won't trust anybody. . . Heck, I won't have them anymore" (*TKM*, p. 274). He finally agrees with Mr. Tate that protecting the fragility of a good man is more important than telling the truth regarding who killed Mr. Ewell. This choice, though extremely difficult, reflects a courageous capacity to see a higher truth which is made possible or at least is aided by a selfless valuing of another human being without being clouded by self-centered emotions, narcissistic rigidities, and self-righteous opinions.

8. Cheerfulness (Good-Spiritedness)

Humility enables us to break out from the prison of the self and consequently frees our spirits, purifies our hearts, and brightens our souls. A humble mode of existence enlivens us, energizes our actions, and recovers our innocence. Like children, our faith in goodness is reinstilled and our eternal hope for the future is reestablished. We are ready to begin again, anew. A selfless orientation toward our world eliminates our illusion of self-importance and makes it possible for us not to take ourselves and our lives too seriously. It opens up our (moral) vision. It enables us to see the comical side of life. It awakens our humorous consciousness and motivates our playful mode of being and acting in the world. We are empowered to laugh heartily at ourselves—our foibles and failures.

Grounded in selfless respect for reality, cheerfulness is incompatible with a false optimism that is based on self-deception and the denial of reality. Good-spiritedness does not cloud or color our vision to the reality of evil, suffering, and other pains of the world. It simply helps us endure, recover, and restart our lives once more. We are reoriented toward the right path. It points to the light at the end of the dark tunnel. It prevents us from wallowing in resentment or self-pity. It disallows us from turning even our suffering into a narcissistic end in itself, rather than a means to, possibly, a higher and better moral vision and a loving orientation.

Although children are vulnerable, they are at the same time resilient. Their resilience is, at least in part, due to the natural ease with which they switch into a cheerful mood and mode of being with others. In relation to adults, their cheerfulness is contagious. It is a welcome relief from the worries of everyday life. Adults can easily be drawn, if they allow themselves to let go of the serious business of living, into the cheerful space of children. This special space is filled with playfulness, humor, and laughter. In this space, games are played, rituals enacted, and loving bonds strengthened. Children and, especially, adults leave this space rejuvenated and revitalized, even if physically exhausted. As adults, we are always awed by children's amazing ability to forget the terrors and tribulations of the previous day or night and awaken after a good night's sleep, cheery-eyed and ready to take on the world with welcoming arms.

When, in the name of religion, "stern-faced" citizens of Maycomb County criticize the beautifully blazing summer flowers of Miss Maudie Atkinson as an expression of indulgent vanity to her face, she counters with a quotation from the Scripture, "A merry heart maketh a cheerful countenance" (*TKM,* p. 159). To paraphrase a little, a pure heart makes a good-spirited disposition. The *Merriam-Webster Dictionary* defines cheerfulness as "marked by or suggestive of lighthearted ease of mind and spirit." It mentions "brightness," "gladness," "radiance," and "sunnyness" as synonyms for cheerfulness. Murdoch would resonate to these metaphorical descriptions. For her, the sun, with its radiance and, warmth, its enlivening, energizing, and enabling power, is a good metaphor for goodness. The closer we get, inwardly and outwardly, to this metaphorical sun, the nearer we are to goodness. Faith in goodness and our loving orientation, as guides to our striving toward excellence (perfection) in word and deed, move us closer to the sun and allows us to experience its brightness and warmth in our lives. We are glad and grateful to be graced with life and to participate in its perfectibility.

After Atticus decides in favor of protecting the vulnerable lifestyle of Boo Radley over exposing him as the one who killed Mr. Bob Ewell to save the lives of Scout and Jem, he conveys his excruciatingly difficult decision to Scout. Scout senses that her father "needed *cheering* up" (*TKM*, p. 276; emphasis added). She runs to him and hugs and kisses him with all her strength and assures him that she understands his decision. She tells him that to expose Mr. Arthur would be like killing an innocent mockingbird. Atticus had once mentioned that it is a sin to kill a mockingbird, and Miss Maudie explained, because mockingbirds bring no harm and only joy to our lives. Atticus is moved by the depth of his daughter's understanding. "Atticus put his face in my hair and rubbed it. When he got up and walked across the porch into the shadows, his *youthful step had returned*" (*TKM*, p. 276; emphasis added). With her attentiveness, imagination, and truth-perceiving intelligence, Scout succeeds in cheering up her father. Atticus is receptive to her mediation and readily returns to his general good-spirited disposition.

Atticus's everyday habits, mannerisms, and general spatiotemporal rhythm (his movements over time) mirror a low-keyed, calm, quiet, and peaceful disposition. Even when disquieting life events intrude, he responds to them "with his infinite capacity for calming turbulent seas" (*TKM*, p. 169). This does not mean he is not affected. He is, but he keeps his emotions under check even when an event like the Tom Robinson case, in the words of his sister, "tears him to pieces" and is wrecking his health (*TKM*, p. 236). In spite of the turmoil in the outside world of Maycomb, Atticus does not draw attention to himself and maintains his faith in the goodness of most people. He exudes a realistic but optimistic outlook even when his life is seen by his family to be in danger. Here Atticus may be perceived by an objective onlooker as innocently naïve to his own detriment. The alternative is to become suspiciously attuned to the mean motives of others, which is incompatible with a good-spirited orientation. Still, there is an overlapping gray area between these alternatives.

In the midst of a tension-filled life situation, Atticus remains caringly focused at home on the concerns and needs of his children. He is able to shift from a serious mode into a playful mode of being with Scout, Jem, and even their friend Dill. When Dill runs away from his home and joins Scout and Jem in a state of hunger and dirt, Atticus, on being called in by Jem, comes to the scene. In learning what has transpired, he comments,

> Atticus's voice had its usual pleasant dryness. "Scout . . You fill this fellow up . . I'm just going over to tell Miss Rachel [Dill's aunt] you're here and ask her if you could spend the night with us—you'd like that, wouldn't you? And for goodness' sake put some of the county back where it belongs, the soil erosion's bad enough as it is."
>
> Dill stared at my father's retreating figure.
>
> "He's tryin' to be funny," I said. "He means take a bath. So there, I told you he wouldn't bother you." (*TKM*, p. 141)

That same evening Scout asks Atticus what "rape" is and later she and Jem get into a fist fight, which deteriorates into a brawl, until they are separated and reconciled by their father. When toward the end of the evening Atticus urges the children to go to bed, he is overheard saying, " 'From rape to riot to runaways,' we heard him chuckle. 'I wonder what the next two hours will bring'" (*TKM*, p. 142). In an earlier episode, Atticus is temporarily persuaded by his sister to press upon his children to behave in ways that match their "background" and "gentle breeding." From his children's reactions he realizes that the stern requirements to behave like the Finches is contrary to the way he has raised them. He reverses himself and calms them. Then,

> He went to the door and out of the room, shutting the door behind him. He nearly slammed it, but caught himself at the last minute and closed it softly. As Jem and I stared, the door opened again and Atticus peered around. His eyebrows were raised, his glasses had slipped. "Get more like Cousin Joshua [who ended up in a mental asylum after attempting unsuccessfully to assassinate the president of the University of Alabama] every day, don't I? Do you think I'll end up costing the family five hundred dollars [the money the Finch family had to pay to get the cousin out]?" (*TKM*, p. 134)

In her book *Feeling and Form,* the philosopher Susanne Langer (1977) comments that "the degree of refinement in individuals may be gauged by what amuses them." What amuses Atticus Finch testifies to his high refinement, good spiritedness, and pure heartedness.

9. Courage

When first viewed side by side, courage and humility may seem contradictory and mutually exclusive. However, this is because typical accounts give us a delimited view of courage and humility. To act selflessly in the service of the other, in spite of seemingly insurmountable obstacles and repellent realities, is the highest form of courage. As a higher-order mode of loving, humble courage encompasses multiple definitions of courage: (1) courage is the determination and the firm resolve to confront, withstand, and overcome threats to one's physical, affective, social, intellectual, and moral integrity; (2) courage is the capacity to experience proper passion; the ability to synthesize or hold in meaningful contiguity polar (opposite) emotions or dispositions; (3) courage is the patience, resoluteness, and resilience needed to be open to that which is different, to be at home with that which is seemingly alien, and to make the unfamiliar familiar. To be courageous is to persist, persevere, and perdure, while being constantly guided by one's moral (loving) vision in spite of life's contingencies, distractions, and pressures. Authentic humility energizes, empowers, and en-*courages* us to make the best of what we have in the selfless service of the other.

The words, actions, and proper passions of Atticus Finch are the exquisite embodiment of moral (physical, emotional, social, and intellectual) courage. He stays selflessly devoted to his children at home in spite of the social pressures that are brought upon him as a result of his vocational commitment and loyalty to the cause of truth, fairness, equality, and human dignity. He remains selflessly respectful of the reality of others even when he is subjected to verbal degradation and physical threats. With controlled passion and unwavering resoluteness, while motivated by his moral (loving) vision, he carries his cross with humble courage. In his own words, courage is "when you know you're licked before you begin but you begin anyway and you see it through no matter what. You rarely win, but sometimes you do" (*TKM*, p. 112). Atticus's daughter, Scout, comes to the realization that her father is "the bravest [most courageous] man who ever lived" upon observing his constant and consistent respectful courteousness toward Mrs. Dubose, who speaks ill of him behind his back and in front of the children who in turn bring it to Atticus's attention (*TKM*, p. 100). Courage requires (is about) such constancy and consistency in conduct across situations and over time. In the words of Miss Maudie Atkinson, "Atticus Finch is the same in his house as he is on the public streets" (*TKM*, p. 46). Atticus himself says, "I can't live one way in town and another way in my home" (*TKM*, p. 274). Interestingly, there is a ritual that Atticus follows which seems to be symbolic of his constancy and consistency. He has cultivated the habit of keeping the same attire on whether he is at work in public or at home in private until bedtime:

> [During the trial] Atticus did something I [Scout] never saw him do before or since, in public or in private: he unbuttoned his vest, unbuttoned his collar, loosened his tie, and took off his coat. He never loosened a scrap of his clothing until he undressed at bedtime, and to Jem and me, this was the equivalent of him standing before us stark naked. (*TKM*, p. 202)

Although there are episodes in *TKM* that demonstrate Atticus's physical courage, such as taking on a mad dog with a "one-shot" gun or taking on a gang which aims at abducting and lynching Tom Robinson from his jail cell without a gun (armed with a newspaper!), Atticus's courage is, above all, moral courage. Turning the other cheek to Mr. Bob Ewell, who verbally degrades Atticus and spits at him, takes a special form of humble courage. Under their father's loving guidance, the children themselves are becoming, day by day, more and more, morally courageous. They are learning how to hold their heads high and be gentle-persons under outside pressures and provocations. Fascinatingly, there is a slow and subtle kind of courage that is being cultivated by the children throughout the unfolding of the novel. It has to do with transforming that which is initially perceived as alien, different, and fear producing into that with which they come to feel at home; to that which becomes familiar; and to that which becomes an object of affinity, trust, and love. Here are some secondary examples: Scout and Jem visit

Calpurnia's African American Church; Scout desires to visit Calpurnia's home to find out how she lives; Scout and Jem invite their classmate, Walter Cunningham, a boy who comes from a poor farming family, to dinner and Scout expresses the desire to befriend him, to her Aunt's chagrin and objection; Scout and Dill talk to Mr. Raymond who is viewed by the townspeople as an evil, eccentric drunkard, only to find out that he is basically a good man. But the primary example is Boo Radley. His slow but subtle transformation, in the eyes of Scout and Jem, from a feared object of curiosity to an object (subject) of love is a reflection of their ripening courage and preocciously acquired wisdom.

10. Wisdom

To be humble is to be wise. Humility and wisdom are enabling virtues. Like the other virtues of love, they overlap and interpenetrate each other. Their slippery meanings subsume each other. Because of wisdom's integrative and pragmatic functions, it requires a special categorization alongside humility. Wisdom involves the translation of perception (knowledge or understanding) into action. Loving wisdom means understanding love's required virtues and applying such (intuitive or explicit) knowledge to everyday life. Wise loving entails practicing daily good habits to the best of one's ability. Wisely loving an object (person or project) according to one's best ability demands accurate awareness and acceptance of one's aptitude (strengths and limitations) and a detailed knowledge of the person or the project at hand. It necessitates making optimal use of one's given gifts, for which one is grateful, in the service of the other. This involves attunement to changing contexts that call for the utilization of one's spontaneous improvisation and ingenuity.

Dictionary definitions, (*Webster's New Collegiate Dictionary,* for instance), offer adjectives to describe wisdom that throw further light on the essential characteristics of the wise person: aware (cognizant; informed), discrete, discerning, insightful, intelligent (makes intelligent choices, conclusions, and decisions), judicious, just (capable of reaching just conclusions), prudent (capable of keeping one's passions, one's actions, oneself under guidance by what one knows to be necessary and right), proper, sagacious (capable of dealing with facts as they apply to everyday life and behavior), sane (level headed and healthy minded in words and deeds), sensible (able to not exceed the dictates of good sense in actions and words), and sound (able to judge accurately relative to what is true and false).

Once more, Atticus Finch personifies the character traits of loving wisdom. He is a man of moderation and prudence. The rhythm of his lifestyle is ordered by rational habits that regulate his momentary emotions and motivations. His calmness and composure modulate his feelings and desires. His predisposition toward moderation creates a balance between his rationality and his passion. Miss Maudie Atkinson conjectures, "if Atticus Finch drank until he was drunk he wouldn't be as hard as some men are at their best" (*TKM*, p. 45). His daughter, Scout, describes her father's habits: "He did not do the things that our schoolmates' fathers did: he never went hunting, he did not play poker or fish or drink or smoke. He sat in the living room and read" (*TKM*, p. 89). Further on, she says, "Our father had a few peculiarities: one was, he never ate desserts; another was that he liked to walk" (*TKM*, p. 148). During times of tension and turmoil, "Atticus subjected every crisis of his life to tranquil evaluation behind" his newspapers (*TKM*, p. 146). And again, Atticus has an "infinite capacity for calming turbulent seas" (*TKM*, p. 169). His eloquent speaking style reflects the attainment of balance between controlled deliberateness and spontaneous straightforwardness. The detached compassion in his voice mirrors his cultivated social sensitivity to his context. He is able to modulate and moderate the degree of passion in his voice to the proper level required by the particular situation he finds himself in.

Wisdom requires that social sensitivity be grounded in conscientiousness, constancy, and consistency. Atticus's conscientiousness is a response to the call of his mature conscience and moral vision, of which he does not lose sight. His constancy shows itself not only in his faithfulness, loyalty, resoluteness, steadfastness, and truthfulness, but also in his authenticity and genuineness. Atticus Finch is what he professes to be. He remains true to his "profession" in word and in deed. As far as consistency is concerned, Scout repeatedly observes that her father is the same at home as he is on the streets of Maycomb.

From their father, Scout and Jem learn the criterion for being good (wise) persons or, in their terms, "fine folks." "Fine folks were people who did the best they could with the sense they had" (*TKM*, p. 130). Certainly, their father is the ideal model who embodies this criterion. He humbly, but optimally, uses his given talents, gratefully, in the service of others—his children, in the service of his community and in the service of humanity.

Atticus is a wisely loving man (in the broadest as well as in the most intimate sense) who understands love's requirements and devotes his life as a parent, lawyer, and citizen to meeting these requisites in practical terms on a daily basis. It is this mission of selfless love that gives his life meaning. Atticus Finch is a man who loves wisely and as such lives morally as well.

4
Parenting as an Existential Life Project

The question What does it mean to be good parents? is part of a larger and more encompassing question: What does it mean to be good persons?[1] The latter is an existential question. But, according to the existential philosopher Michael Gelven, we cannot ask the latter question without asking the correlative question, What does it mean to be bad persons? These two questions go hand in hand. We cannot be good persons without having the potential to be bad persons. Our existential reality is such that we are both potentially both good and bad persons. The potential conflict between being good and being bad is of the essence of our human makeup.

For Gelven, the acquisition of self-awareness and the discovery of our conflictive nature are concurrent developmental processes. Our children unreflectively engage in impulsive behaviors in order to gratify themselves. As parents we say no to some of these behaviors in order to keep them in check. By saying no and reprimanding our children we force them to become aware of the conflicting maxims within themselves. When we tell them "Do not pull the dog's tail," we, as parents, are negatively checking their natural desires for curiosity and mastery. This triggers a conflict within themselves between their drives for curiosity and mastery and their parental concern for the dog.

Inevitably, children experience feelings of anger and rage in response to perceived privations, restrictions, and other mistreatments inflicted on them by parents, siblings, peers, relatives, and strangers. Their outrage is grounded in a founded or unfounded prereflective understanding that they have been wronged or that they have been unfairly or unjustly treated. Their natural immediate impulse is to seek redress and to right the wrong. How they learn to go about seeking redress and righting the wrong is part of learning to become good. When children feel that they are unable to seek redress or right the wrong, they feel helpless and impotent. In such a context, they are left with the options of either turning against themselves or turning against other vulnerable, available, and visible targets on whom they displace their pent-up frustrations and aggressions. Or, they may use both self- and other-destructive strategies. The seeds of sado-masochistic impulses are sown. Here is where judicious parental mediation is critical. Parents who are fair, firm, flexible, and affectionate enable and empower their children to confront their own badness having acquired a primordial faith in their own goodness and in the goodness of their parents. Under the just and loving gaze of their parents and other essential figures in their lives, children gain the moral strength to resist wrongdoing with being good. They also gain the moral courage to seek redress for being wronged. They learn that to be good is to be just.

As concerned and caring parents, we want our children to become good persons, to develop into noble and wholesome characters. In order to become good characters, they need to learn to confront their potentiality for being bad. They cannot be good without their potential for being bad. Becoming a good person requires a constant struggle to overcome the ever-present possibility of wrongdoing or the committing of evilish acts.

According to Gelven, becoming a good person can only take place against the backdrop of having acquired and taken for granted a deep sense of belongingness. Our children need to feel that they belong to a family. Their home is, or ought to be, their second womb. They need to feel welcome in their own home. Ideally, as the parameters of home expand, there is also a parallel widening of welcome. They learn to be at home and welcome in the world.

When Gelven says that goodness emerges from a primordial ground of belongingness, he means that children need to belong to something larger than themselves in order to feel good about themselves and in order to be and become good persons. It is not accidental that parents say lovingly to their child, "You are a part of me; you are my flesh and blood; you belong to me!" The feeling of belonging, of being warmly welcomed, of being at home is a requisite for experiencing inner goodness and for the development of good character.

The opposite also upholds. The feeling of not belonging, of being unwelcome, of not being at home—of being alien or foreign, is a precondition for feeling bad within or being a bad character. It is what makes possible the experiencing of self-disgust, self-exile, self-loathing, and self- or other-directed rage. It corrupts character.

Gelven distinguishes between personality and character. Personality is a by-product of genetic (inherited) and environmental (especially early familial) influences. Character is cultivated from within. It is the by-product of consciously adopted attitudes, habits, and ways of thinking pursued for the purpose of becoming the kind of persons we envision we ought to become. Although our character is influenced by our personality, it is at the same time functionally autonomous. Character is of the essence of our authentic Selfhood. We, in a significant part, determine our own character. We have a voice in guiding our own becoming. To be bad is to allow our genetic or environmental influences to distract us from developing our good character. Being bad is deviating from pursuing the path of integrity.

In order for us to develop good character, we need to become virtuous. For Gelven, becoming virtuous is equivalent to a special kind of (moral) learning. It is not the kind of learning that refers to gaining information or knowledge. It is learning to become a certain kind of person. Practicing a vice is learning to become a bad character. Practicing a virtue is learning to become a good character. Our character is the seat of our virtues and vices.

Learning to become a bad person or a corrupt character is a gradual process that involves self-deception, distraction, indifference, self-justification, and ultimately blind submission. This process precedes, accompanies, or follows the practice of vices, which is a form of bad learning. Being human, we are all capable of being bad parents. It is this reality that enables us to be good parents. The aim is not the eradication of (potential) badness; rather, it is the vigilant keeping of our potential for badness in check. We are both good and bad parents. Becoming good parents involves confronting and overcoming our being bad parents.

Our children, too, are only capable of being good when they become capable of being bad. Before this awareness surfaces, they are simply unaware. Gelven describes this as a state of innocent ignorance.[2] As they are socialized, they become aware of their conflictive nature: that they are good and bad. They become aware of the dynamic tension within them. They are forced to reflect on and contain their badness in order to be good.

As parents, it is our hope that our children turn toward becoming good characters and turn away from becoming bad characters. Guided by their human reality, they, like us, are equipped with the positive power to be good and the negative power to be bad. The positive power to be good has an independent authority of its own. It is through the cultivation of the positive power (energy) of goodness that they are enabled to neutralize the negative power (energy) of badness. The environment we create for them, on a familial and societal level, contributes to either the clearing or the obstruction of the path toward achieving goodness.

As we have seen in chapter 3, the goodness of Atticus Finch's character ennobles the moral landscape of his familial and communal lived space. In contradistinction to Atticus's character, the bad character of Robert E. Lee Ewell contaminates not only his familial grounds, but also the grounds of Maycomb County. Incidentally, it is not accidental that the location of Ewell's residence is placed next to the town garbage dump. Nevertheless, in spite of the pervasiveness of the perverse in the Ewell household, Harper Lee brings to the reader's attention the presence of beautiful red geraniums in the midst of physical, interpersonal, and moral ugliness. These geraniums, which are symbolic of the ever-present possibility of goodness, are thriving under the caring hands of Mayella Violet Ewell.

The corruption of Bob Ewell's character is revealed in the collapse of resistance to the allure of all temptations. He practices the bad habits of chewing tobacco and drinking alcohol, as well as verbally, physically, and even sexually abusing his children. Like their father, the children are unclean, mean, and vindictive. In contrast, the nobility of Atticus Finch's character radiates with dignity and integrity that shine through the demeanor of his children. The reader's resonance to the beauty of Atticus's character attests to the universality of the truth that is reflected through the light of his goodness. Whereas Atticus's character mirrors nobility (goodness), Bob Ewell's character mirrors corruption (badness). For Gelven, it is this mirroring that constitutes our character. In Atticus Finch and Bob Ewell, Harper Lee is presenting to us the two opposite and conflicting sides of our human reality: the Christlike figure versus the Satanlike figure.

Atticus's character is "characterized" by mirroring who he is in truth. He treasures and respects the truth that is reflected through him. He guards what makes him special and unique with unwavering tenacity. Paradoxically, what he holds as precious requires of him selflessness and self-sacrifice in order to keep himself intact and integrated, to maintain his sense of integrity. Who he is, the kind of person he is, and the truth that he embodies and is mirrored through him, all matter to him. This holding on to and guarding what matters to him is what "characterizes" him. Becoming who he is, however, is grounded in his unshakable sense of belonging. "He liked Maycomb, he was Maycomb County born and bred; he knew his people, they knew him" (*TKM,* p. 5). More than this, he has an abiding sense that he is a part of a larger organismic whole. In spite of his trials and tribulations, and even though he is blessed with exceptional intelligence and talents, he never separates himself from the humanity to which he belongs. He is always able to step back, reflect on that which he wants to hold on to dearly—his family, the larger whole of which he is a part, and the truth which he lives by and bodies forth.

Through serving as an example, through teaching, guidance, and encouragement, Atticus imparts what "characterizes" him to his children. Scout and Jem are made to feel special and unique. At the same time they are encouraged to become selfless and self-sacrificing. Even in the midst of imminent danger to himself and his family, Atticus reminds his sister that Maycomb is the children's home and that once the storm settles down, it will remain their dwelling place. A lesson that is repeated in the Finch household is that through empathic imagination we discover the humanity in all of us; we tolerate, accept, and are respectful of differences.

Becoming good parents requires the development of good character in ourselves and in our children. Our character can be described as the ratio of our virtues to our vices. Virtues and vices are good and bad ways of learning to confront our intrapersonal, interpersonal, and existential modalities of our finite existence. More concretely, there are ways of learning to love and suffer well or badly. There are ways of learning to confront our loneliness rightly or wrongly. We can learn to come to terms with our strengths and limitations constructively or destructively. There are good and bad ways of handling our fatigue, hunger, sleeplessness, and physical pain. There are different ways of responding to the repellent realities of others and to their own and our own imperfections. In a Christlike manner, Atticus Finch practices and encourages his children to practice turning the other cheek in response to the verbal assaults of those who object to the stance he has taken to defend the human rights of a good and innocent man.

Although initially, Jem and, especially, Scout, respond through aggressive means to such provocations, they learn, under their father's guidance and encouragement, to hold their head high in such circumstances. In contrast to Scout and Jem, Burris, the son of Bob Ewell, attributes hostile intentions to his first-grade teacher, where none exist, in response to her concern about his state of uncleanliness. When she advises him to go home and follow her hygenic prescriptions, he responds, when he is safely at the classroom door, by shouting, "Report and be damned to ye! Ain't no snot-nosed slut of a schoolteacher ever born c'n make me do nothin'! You ain't makin' me go nowhere, missus. You just remember that, you ain't makin' me go nowhere!" (*TKM,* p. 28).

From a Gelvenian perspective, the nobility or corruption of our character is mirrored through how well or badly we learn to confront our fears and temptations, our unanswered wrongs, our ignorance, our sense of the infinite (that which is larger than ourselves), and our own selves. Being courageous requires learning to confront our fears and temptations. Being just involves learning to confront our unanswered wrongs. Becoming wise means learning to confront our ignorance. Learning to be reverent in the presence of that which is larger than ourselves is to become pious. To be noble is to learn to confront ourselves.

To become a virtuous character requires the practice of excellence. Practice is a part of the process of learning. For Gelven, learning is of the essence of virtue. This is not, however, learning in the sense of acquiring information or knowledge. It is learning to become who we are. It is learning to be the kind of persons we can become. It is learning to become the best persons we can be. It is learning to embody and mirror goodness from the inside out and outside in. It is to partake of and be a conduit for universal goodness. At the same time, this kind of learning is characterized by being intensely individualistic. As illustrated in chapter 3, Atticus Finch is a beautiful exemplar of the noble character. He practices excellence in his everyday life. His character is a concrete embodiment of universal goodness. As a good character, he is a reflector of universal virtues with which readers across the world identify and to which they resonate. At the same time his character bears his unique individual style.

Gelven distinguishes between good learning and bad learning. Good learning ennobles our character. Bad learning or the failure to learn corrupts our character. Through (existential) learning we become who we are. In Harper Lee's *To Kill a Mockingbird,* Atticus Finch teaches his children about courage, justice, wisdom (good judgment), piety, and nobility. Through his example, mentorship, and loving guidance, through the children's own imaginative and playful initiatives, and through their observation of and participation in the unfolding life drama surrounding them, Scout and Jem are learning to confront, constructively and creatively, their fears and temptations, their unanswered wrongs, their limited knowledge, their sense of the mysterious, and, lastly, their own Selfhood. They are learning to become good by confronting that which is bad within and outside themselves.

Scout and Jem are learning to be morally courageous when they acquire the capacity to resist the temptation to fight back, retaliate, and take revenge. It is this kind of learning which keeps them from practicing the same cruelty of other children and adults in their community. They are also becoming morally courageous by learning to confront their fears. The fear of the unknown or that which is different is a dominant theme throughout the novel. Boo Radley, a neighbor who is a ghostlike figure, is an object of fear and fascination for the children. Even the nickname, Boo, connotes fear. In their attempt to confront their fear of this alien, different, and hidden entity, Scout and Jem, along with their friend Dill, construct playful dramas which depict imaginatively the world of Boo Radley and the inner workings of his mind. They also initiate futile attempts at communicating with him. They embark on these projects with simultaneous apprehension and irresistible attraction and to the intermittent chagrin and objection of Atticus. Yet, it is Boo who anonymously places gifts for them in a tree hole. It is Boo who mends the torn pants of Jem who left them behind while escaping the Radley property. And ultimately, it is Boo who saves Scout and Jem from being killed by Bob Ewell. Toward the end of the novel, this fear-inspiring figure is embraced and absorbed into the expanding identity of the children as a friendly, fatherlike, loving figure. Here is Scout engaging in intimate reflection as she stands alone on the Radley porch having been "escorted" by Boo Radley from her home:

> Boo was our neighbor. He gave us two soap dolls, a broken watch and chain, a pair of good-luck pennies, and our lives. But neighbors give in return. We never put back into the tree what we took out of it: we had given him nothing, and it made me sad . . . [When Autumn came] and Boo's children needed him [he was there to save them]. Atticus was right. One time he said you never really know a man until you stand in his shoes and walk around in them. Just standing on the Radley porch was enough. (*TKM,* pp. 278–79)

It is interesting to note that this type of intimate reflection or reflective intimacy is, for Gelven, essential for the process of integration, of becoming an integrated whole.

Scout has prepared, imaginatively, for this ultimate encounter with Boo Radley:

> Maybe someday we would see him. I imagined how it would be: when it happened he'd just be sitting there in the swing when I came along. "Hidy do, Mr. Arthur," I would say, as if I had said it every afternoon of my life. "Evening, Jean Louise," he would say, as if he had said it every afternoon of my life, "right pretty spell we're having, isn't it?" "Yes sir, right pretty," I would say, and go on. It was only a fantasy. (*TKM,* p. 242)

This openness to the seemingly alien, new, and different characterizes the children's emerging personhood. Scout and Jem welcome the opportunity to visit

Calpurnia's church. Jem invites Walter Cunningham for dinner. Scout wants to invite him to stay overnight, to the vehement objection of her Aunt Alexandra. Aunt Alexandra explains, " 'I'll tell you why,' she said. 'Because he—is—trash, that's why you can't play with him, picking up his habits and learning Lord—knows—what' " (*TKM*, p. 225). Similarly, Aunt Alexandra opposes Scout's "plans to visit Calpurnia's house—I was curious, interested; I wanted to be her 'company,' to see how she lived, who her friends were" (*TKM*, p. 224). Although Atticus attempts not to undermine his sister's authority in the eyes of the children, he steers the delicate course of <u>affirming their courageous willingness to reach out</u> <u>and integrate into their experience that which is new and different, while at the</u> <u>same time protecting and preparing them for the challenges and dangers of the</u> <u>real world.</u>

After accompanying Boo Radley to his house and engaging in intimate reflection on the Radley porch, Scout returns home to find her father, Atticus, in "Jem's room, sitting by his bed. He was reading a book" (*TKM*, p. 280). Upon discovering that Atticus is reading Seckatary Hawkins's *The Gray Ghost*, Scout asks him,

> "Read it aloud, please, Atticus. It's real scary."
> "No," he said. "You've had enough scaring for awhile. This is too—"
> "Atticus, I wasn't scared."
> He raised his eyebrows, and I protested: "Leastaways not till I started telling Mr. Tate about it. Jem wasn't scared. Asked him and he said he wasn't. Besides, *nothin's real scary except in books.*"
> Atticus opened his mouth to say something, but shut it again. He took his thumb from the middle of the book and turned back to the first page. (*TKM*, p. 280; emphasis added)

Scout is here giving expression to her coming to terms, not only with her traumatic encounter with Bob Ewell, but more importantly, to her encounter with Boo Radley. Boo, who is a figure of fear at the beginning of the novel, is now, at the end of the novel, a friendly father figure.

The children, Scout and Jem, are learning from their father the lived meaning of courage. Through this kind of learning, they are becoming who they are. Through his guidance and example, they are learning how to confront life's burdens and fearsome challenges. They are learning how to be noble characters like their father. Learning to become noble, through being courageous, requires practicing resistance to the lure of temptations. To illustrate, Atticus lectures Scout about using her head instead of her fists in response to unjust provocations from her classmates. "And the sooner I *learned to hold in,* the better everybody would be" (*TKM*, p. 74; emphasis added). Upon next succeeding in "holding in" and holding her head high by remembering what her father had said and not wanting to let him down, she feels "extremely *noble* for having remembered" (*TKM*, p. 77; emphasis added).

Atticus does not succumb to the threats or burdens of life, which are not greater but lesser than himself. By not succumbing to their influence, his character is ennobled. In resisting their influence, he gains moral strength. The nobility of his character lies, at least in an important part, in his capacity to resist the lure of temptations. But it is not a by-product of a single act of courage. His entire life history leads up to it. In other words, he has been practicing his practical virtues over the course of his lifetime. His courage lies in the triumph of his moral strength over the allure of the potentially weakening temptations, which, for Atticus, would be a source of cowardice and shame.

Atticus conducts himself in such a way so as he has nothing to be ashamed of; so that he can look his children in the eye and ask them, with a clear conscience, to do something; so that he can hold his head high in town; so that he can represent his county in the legislature. Atticus has nothing to hide. The hidden (invisible) is made radiantly visible in the carriage of his character. He does not hide or turn away from confronting troubling circumstances. He does not hide or turn away from his own truth. Being courageous requires not hiding but turning toward, and acting in accordance with one's own truth.

In contradistinction to the character of Atticus Finch, Bob Ewell leads an entire life of indolence. He avoids his moral exercising. His moral weakness is a form of cowardice. Ewell refuses to face his shameful past. By not confronting his shameful past he is being cowardly. By being shameless, by not confronting himself at all, he is closing himself to the possibility of redemption. Shame can be redemptive only if it is confronted. His shameless lifestyle is made possible by turning away from such confrontation. He shamelessly refuses to look into his present or past shameful ways. By not confronting his shame, he blinds himself to the paradoxical truth that strength emerges from facing one's weakness. Instead, his unfaced shame is transformed into and shows itself through his self-indulgence, perverse selfishness, smallness, ugliness, self-pity, insolent arrogance, and impotent rage. He is at once a victimizer (of the powerless) who feels victimized by the powerful.

Atticus courageously confronts the ultimate challenge of his professional life. He takes on the task of defending an innocent black man, Tom Robinson, who is accused of rape by a white man, Bob Ewell, and his daughter, Mayella Ewell. Atticus is willing to face the challenge regardless of the probability of success, which is very small. Although winning the case matters to Atticus, emerging from the struggle with his integrity intact matters more. His integrity constitutes an essential part of the struggle as a whole. Who he is, the kind of person he is, matters in this whole struggle. He is a part of a struggle that matters. He does care about succeeding, but he does not depend on it for the maintenance of his moral worth. He is not only concerned about the strong likelihood of failure, but, more than that, he is fearful about the ramifications of his active role upon his children. This, however, does not detract or distract him from investing his energy and doing his best to defend Tom Robinson. His integrity is at stake.

Atticus's courageous sacrifice is not made simply for personal satisfaction or private gain. He endures the pain and stress of his struggle for the sake of that which is larger than himself. He is sacrificing his personal gain for the sake of the valued principles of the institution of the law, which he regards with reverence and awe. He is willing to sacrifice his private advantage in order not to violate his sacred sense of belongingness to his own family, community, religion, and human family. Simply stated, Atticus is willing to confront life's anxiety-producing and fearsome challenges and threats and to sacrifice his personal interest for the sake of Goodness. He is simultaneously affirming the good within himself and the Good outside himself (Universal Goodness). He is, at once, affirming his own personal calling or special meaning in life and his reverence for the Good itself.

Part of Atticus's courage lies in his resistance of the impulse to transfer his suffering role onto his vulnerable children. Even while undergoing extreme pressures and being subjected to seemingly unbearable tension-producing stressors, he maintains his calm, patient, and loving attitude toward his children. His sister, Alexandra, describes his state, "It tears him to pieces. He doesn't show it much, but it tears him to pieces. I've seen him when—what else do they want from him?" (*TKM*, p. 236). Still, he is not perfect. He is not totally able to maintain his compassionate detachment and benevolent neutrality in the face of his sister's persistent opposition to his principled stance. Scout, the narrator, states, "I was beginning to notice a subtle change in my father these days, that came out when he talked with Aunt Alexandra. It was a quiet digging in, never outright irritation" (*TKM*, p. 157).

Atticus's courage is contagious. His children catch the contagion. In a moving moment in Harper Lee's novel, Scout and Jem come to the defense of their father when he is threatened by a mob for standing in their way in their attempt to abduct and lynch Tom Robinson. Here is how Scout confronts the fearsome situation:

> I sought once more for a familiar face, and at the center of the semi-circle I found one.
> "Hey, Mr. Cunningham [a poor client-farmer of her father's]. . . . Don't you remember me, Mr. Cunningham? I'm Jean Louise Finch. You brought us some hickory nuts one time [in partial payment for her father's legal services, as he lacked the financial resources to make a direct payment], remember?" I began to sense the futility one feels when unacknowledged by a chance acquaintance. "I go to school with Walter [Mr. Cunningham's son]," I began again. "He's your boy, ain't he? Ain't he, sir?"
> Mr. Cunningham was moved to a faint nod. He did know me, after all.
> "He's in my grade," I said, "and he does right well. He's a *good boy*," I added "a real nice boy. We brought him home for dinner one time. Maybe he told you about me, I beat him up one time but he was real nice about it. Tell him hey for me, won't you?"

. . .

I looked around and up at Mr. Cunningham, whose face was equally impassive. Then he did a peculiar thing. He squatted down and took me by both shoulders. "I'll tell him you said hey, little lady," he said.

Then he straightened up and waved a big paw. "Let's clear out," he called. Let's get going boys." (*TKM*, pp. 153–54; emphasis added)

Innocently and instinctively, Scout appeals to Walter Cunningham's humanity and goodness. She forces him to see her, her father, and thus the situation from a human, heartfelt perspective. He revisions the unfolding drama from the viewpoint of a father of a vulnerable child and a child who is courageously protecting her father who has been good to him. The following morning, at the breakfast table, Atticus comments,

"Mr. Cunningham's basically a *good man*," he said, "he just has his blind spots along with the rest of us."

. . .

"A mob's always made up of people, no matter what. Mr. Cunningham was part of a mob last night, but he was still a man . . . ."

"So it took an eight-year-old child to bring 'em to their senses, didn't it?" said Atticus. "That proves something—that a gang of wild animals *can* be stopped, simply because they're still human. Hmp, maybe we need a police force of children. . . . you children last night made Mr. Cunningham stand in my shoes for a minute. That was enough." (*TKM*, p. 157; emphasis added)

The cowardice of parents is also contagious. Bob Ewell's children absorb their father's cowardliness. Ewell, like the other Ewells that have come before him, refuses to confront the challenge of earning an honest living. "Atticus said the Ewells had been the disgrace of Maycomb for three generations. None of them had done an honest day's work in his recollection" (*TKM*, p. 30). And in Sheriff Tate's assessment,

"[Bob Ewell] wasn't crazy, mean as hell. Low-down skunk with enough liquor in him to make him brave enough to kill children."

. . .

"Mr. Finch, there's just some kind of men you have to shoot before you can say hidy to 'em. Ewell's one of 'em.

. . .

"He had guts enough to pester a poor colored woman [Tom Robinson's wife], he had guts enough to pester Judge Taylor when he thought the house was empty, so do you think he'da met you to your face in daylight?" (*TKM*, p. 269)

The father-daughter collusion in not facing their shameful present and past and in accusing an innocent and vulnerable black man who extends a helping hand to the daughter is itself an act of cowardliness. Cowardliness corrupts character. It is an obstacle to the achievement of good character. It is incompatible with the actualization of true Selfhood. It alienates from genuine communal belongingness. Atticus describes how Judge Taylor views Bob Ewell on the witness stand: "John looked at him as if he was a three-legged chicken or a square egg" (*TKM,* p. 250). And when Link Deas, Helen Robinson's employer, warns Bob Ewell not to bother his cook, Helen, Bob Ewell responds, "Don't you look at me, Link Deas, like I was dirt" (*TKM,* p. 249).

Being good parents requires of us to be just parents. But being good parents necessitates the occasional bracketing of justice in order to forgive in the name of love. We forgive a misdeed or a wrongdoing on the part of our children, even though in all fairness they deserve punishment, because we love them. Whereas just punishment aims at the act, love aims at the whole person. In a loving home or a caring environment, justice is tempered by mercy and forgiveness, which preserve and protect a sacred sense of belongingness. In the name of goodness, we are willing to forgive each other because we lovingly belong to each other.

The Finch home is a just place of dwelling. That Atticus is an affectionate, fair, firm, and flexible parent has been touched on in chapter 3. The spirit of forgiveness also permeates the household. Scout forgives her uncle after he punishes her physically for her altercation with her cousin without listening to her side of the story, which he subsequently does. Atticus practices forgiveness and urges his children to do the same, toward those who have attempted to hurt and harm him verbally or even physically. He wants to forgive these unanswered wrongs in order to preserve that valued sense of belongingness to the community. Scout and Jem appropriate from their father not only the virtue of justice but also the complementary virtue of forgiveness.

In contrast to the noble character of Atticus Finch, the corrupt character of Bob Ewell is incapable of the complementary virtues of justice and forgiveness. He is unfair and unloving toward his children, whom he mistreats physically, and, in the case of his daughter Mayella, sexually. His house is characterized by chaos, disorder, filth, and tyranny. He spends his welfare checks on liquor, while his children are left hungry and alone to fend for themselves. He hunts out of season, violating state laws. He collects his welfare checks without honestly seeking a job. His children are truants who run around without adult supervision and guidance. Instead of confronting his temptations constructively, he gives in to them to gratify his own impulsive needs. He does not engage in potentially redemptive reflections. Instead, he acts blindly and habitually, guided by shallow self-deceptive justifications and rationalizations. He consistently violates the dignity and sanctity of his own children. He desecrates the sacredness of his familial and communal belongingness. As an abhorrent character, he finds himself unwelcome in his community. He does not belong. He is exiled. He is at the same time in self-exile. And as a corrupt character, he lacks the capacity for forgiveness. In spite of the fact that he has falsely accused Tom Robinson of raping his daughter Mayella, Bob Ewell aims to hurt those who came to his defense. As a cowardly man who lacks a sense of fairness, he either attempts or succeeds in harming and hurting vulnerable others in his social surrounding: his own children, Tom Robinson (a one-armed black man who felt sorry for Mayella and thus offered her assistance), Tom Robinson's wife (as a widowed woman), and Atticus Finch's children, Scout and Jem.

Growing up in an unloving home, Mayella Violet Ewell lacks the capacity to love. When Atticus asks her in court, "Do you love your father, Miss Mayella?" she responds, "love him, whatcha mean?" (*TKM*, p. 183). Like her father, Mayella is incapable of fairness or forgiveness. She colludes with her father in accusing Tom Robinson of raping her. Through a self-deceptive mental maneuver she comes to hate and wish the ultimate punishment for the only man who has been kind to her. This is done in an effort to counter her fleeting sense of guilt and shame for having attempted to tempt a young, married black man, although the initial reaching out for his assistance may have been an innocent and healthy impulse to move outside and away from her decadent and confining household.

Good parents, on the whole, make good judgments. Being human, and thus imperfect, they also make bad judgments. But when they make bad judgments, they are willing to confront their judgmental failures and learn from their mistakes. They realize that their judgments reflect the kind of persons they are. The way parents make judgments is an index of their character.

According to Gelven, making good judgments involves putting things together in a cohesive, revealing, and synthesizing way. To make bad judgments is to put things together in a distortive way. When we read our situation well, we make good judgments. When we misread out situation, we make bad judgments. Good judgments bring about good order; bad judgments bring about disorder.

The way we judge others, or the way we make judgments about our world in general, goes hand in hand with the way we make judgments about ourselves. To judge wisely is to place ourselves properly in the scheme of things. To judge unwisely is to misplace ourselves in the scheme of things. It is to distort our self-importance. This is a form of self-misjudgment. It disallows for genuine self-acceptance. It falsifies our power in a self-serving manner.

The character of Bob Ewell illustrates well the processes of self-misjudgment in particular and bad judgment in general. He embodies the twisted traits of arrogance, pomposity, and false pride that derive from a distorted sense of self-importance. Although he lives in a dilapidated cabin behind the town garbage dump, he sees it as beneath him to be in close proximity to Tom Robinson. He tells Judge Taylor while on the witness stand, "Jedge I've asked this county for fifteen years to clean out that nest down yonder, they're dangerous to live around 'sides devaluin' my property" (*TKM*, p. 175). The narrator, Scout, describes his initial appearance, "a little bantam cock of a man," as having "no resemblance to his namesake" (*TKM*, pp. 169–70). It is with ironic intent that the author names him Robert E. Lee Ewell, after a well-known Southern Confederate general. The cock image is an apt description of Ewell's tendency toward self-inflation:

> The little man seemed to have forgotten his previous humiliation from the bench. It was becoming evident that he thought Atticus an easy match. He seemed to grow ruddy again; his chest swelled, and once more he was a red little rooster. (*TKM*, p. 176)

An unconscious self-transformation has occurred in Ewell's self-judging eyes from not mattering to mattering out of proportion to his proper place in the community of which he is a part. He is alienated from his own humanity. Through his self-deception, he has succeeded in silencing the voice that judges his distorted self-judgment and his capacity for judgment making. He has also "inherited" a familial tradition of bad judgment making, which he is passing on to his own children. The narrator says:

> [T]he Ewells lived as guests of the county in prosperity as well as in the depths of depression. No truant officers could keep their numerous offspring in school; no public health officer could free them from congenital defects, various worms, and the diseases indigenous to filthy surroundings. (*TKM*, p. 170)

As mentioned earlier, "Atticus said the Ewells had been the disgrace of Maycomb for three generations. None of them had done an honest day's work in his recollection" (*TKM*, p. 30). Subsequent to the conviction of Tom Robinson and his death, while attempting to escape from prison,

> Mr. Bob Ewell acquired and lost a job in a matter of days and probably made himself unique in the annals of the nineteen-thirties: he was the only man I [Scout, the narrator] ever heard of who was fired from the WPA for laziness. I suppose his brief burst of fame brought on a briefer burst of industry, but his job lasted only as long as his notoriety: Mr. Ewell found himself as forgotten as Tom Robinson. Thereafter, he resumed his regular weekly appearances at the welfare office for his check, and received it with no grace and obscure mutterings that the bastards who ran this town wouldn't permit an honest man to make a living. (*TKM*, p. 248)

Now, for Gelven, to judge is to fit the (existential) elements in one's world either badly or well. In the above episode, the elements in Bob Ewell's world are: self-importance, entitlement, the need for attention, the need to make a living (survival), the self/societal expectation of effort and industry, the impulse toward inertia and laziness, the need to maintain the semblance of dignity (dignified honesty), and the sense of being limited (oppressed) by powerful authorities and institutions. Ewell's bad judgment lies in fitting these elements together in an incoherent way. From this forced fitting, he derives the conclusion that it is those who are in positions of power, such as Atticus Finch, who are depriving an honest man like him from making a living. This bad fitting of the elements is made possible by habitual self-deception, denial, and the silencing of the inner voice of truth. Even if the sense of oppression is valid, which in this instance it is not, it can be used in bad faith and in a self-serving manner to justify immoral conduct.

Good judgment, according to Gelven, requires the primacy of the whole over the parts (the elements). Bad judgment results from the dominance of one or more of the parts over the whole. For example, when a parent judges himself as a "father" (an element) in terms of his devotion to his daughter, he is reading his "being a father" in terms of "being a family," which is the broader context (whole). But if a father judges his family in terms of his status as a "father," which is the reverse process, he is making a bad judgment. For Gelven, this is an impious or irreverent act which stands in the way of becoming integrated and belonging to a greater whole. When Bob Ewell, as a father, spends his relief checks on whiskey and goes off to the swamp for days and lets his children fend for themselves and go hungry, he is making a bad judgment. In his world, the part (his own narcissistic needs or he himself) comes before the whole (his family).

From Gelven's point of view, bad judgment making is a by-product of bad learning, the failure to learn, or the cessation of learning. Again, by (existential) learning, he means learning to become who we are as persons (characters). The failure to learn has to do with the failure to confront our own ignorance or lack of knowledge. It has further to do with our fear of the unknown and the unknowable, fear of failure, and fear of our own effort and initiative. It is related to our unwillingness to face our self-distractions, self-deceptions, and self-betrayals. It involves not being able to laugh at ourselves and learn from our mistakes. We stop learning when we take ourselves too seriously; when, guided by a sense of false pride, we exaggerate our self-importance. We are unable to learn when we fail to embrace our foolishness and finitude: our limitations, frailties, and fragilities.

The ability to learn, according to Gelven, is the foundation of all virtues. To be unable to learn, therefore, is the basis of all vices. It is good for children to learn. It is bad for children to fail to learn or to stop learning. Learning is essential to goodness. It is this kind of learning that is equivalent to the acquisition of wisdom. Becoming wise consists, among other things, learning to make good judgments, learning to be fair and just, and learning to be courageous. Learning, is, therefore, essential to becoming a good character.

Harper Lee's *To Kill a Mockingbird* can now be viewed as a story about how two children, Scout and Jem, are learning to become good characters. It is a narrative about a good father, a single parent, who, as a mentor and model, contributes optimally to the character development of his two children. Interestingly, the author contrasts the true, effective, (existential) learning of the children to the false, informational learning of the official educational system. The narrating Scout reflects on her public school experience:

> The remainder of my schooldays were no more auspicious than the first. . . . [A]s I inched sluggishly along the treadmill of the Maycomb County school system, I could not help receiving the impression that I was being cheated out of something. Out of what I knew not, yet I did not believe that twelve years of unrelieved boredom was exactly what the state had in mind for me. (*TKM*, p. 32)

Scout and Jem are learning the truth: they are learning to be good human beings. Partaking of the beauty of goodness is the ultimate truth of the novel. But, learning to become good, they discover, entails coming to terms with the badness within and around them. It necessitates enduring that which is unpleasant and painful. The road to goodness contains suffering along the way. The reader cannot escape noticing the children's precocious and resilient capacity for authentic learning. Among other virtues, they are learning and practicing the virtues of courage, justice, and wisdom. As readers, we "see" their character develop in a virtuous way. We observe the development of their good character. We witness the triumph of (their) goodness over (but not the elimination of) badness (evil). For without (perpetual confrontation with) badness, there can be no goodness. By learning and practicing the virtues of courage, justice, and good judgment, Scout and Jem are slowly but surely approximating the nobility of their father's character in their own most personal and unique ways. Through this kind of true learning, they are becoming their own persons. They are becoming most at home with themselves and in the world. In becoming good, they are achieving a sense of being welcome—a sense of their own precious presence, in the world. At the same time, they are acquiring a reverence for a larger presence: the light of the truth of goodness.

5
Empowerment in Parenting

According to Rollo May, human consciousness operates through polarities.[1] Built into the structure of our consciousness is a back-and-forth movement between opposites. For instance, developing children will not be truly able to say their own yes until they have given ample expression to their no-saying. Saying no plays a critical role in how they come to say yes. Negation is a requisite for affirmation. How parents handle the no-saying phase of their developing children will have influence on the quality of their children's authoritative yes-saying. Children's consciousness, therefore, grows out of this constant interplay and interaction between its polar tendencies. Good parents are sensitively attuned to their children's natural movement between the polarities of existence: negation versus affirmation, dependence versus independence, moving toward others versus moving away from others, maturity versus immaturity, self-awareness versus self-forgetfulness, and so on.

For May, as he is freely interpreted for the purposes of this project, there are two fundamental, bipolar, and dialectically interrelated modalities of consciousness. We will label them as *integrative power* versus *disintegrative power*. Paradoxically, from an existential perspective, these modalities of consciousness or ways of being in the world are not only opposites, but they also require and are absorbed into one another. They are simultaneously biologically based and have existential significance for our lives, for how we exist or who and how we are in the world *YANG +* *YIN* with others.

May reminds us that the "word power comes from the Latin *posse,* meaning 'to be able'" (May, 1972, p. 19). In one sense, power means "the ability to cause or prevent change" (May, 1972, p. 99). However, May attributes multiple meanings to power, especially when it fuses with pleasure as it is broadly understood. Children are born gifted with the power to be and become who they are partly free and partly destined to be. For May, power (empowerment) and freedom are interrelated concepts. "Freedom is the *power* to mold and create ourselves. Freedom is the capacity . . . 'to become what we truly are'" (May, 1953, p. 165; emphasis added). "Freedom is the possibility of development, of enhancement of one's life" (May, 1981, p. 5). Good parenting, therefore, involves empowering children in order to enable them to become who they truly are. Parents, however, are cautioned against pseudoempowerment. Parents who tell their children that they can be or become anything or anyone they want to be are in reality disempowering their children. They are not being realistic about their children's limitations and competencies. "One is free only as one recognizes one's limits" (May, 1981, p. 158). When parents deny their children's limitations or assets, they are making it difficult for children to be themselves. "There is no denying talents (and limitations) without penalty, and one name for that attempt is neurosis" (May, 1981, p. 90).

As has been mentioned earlier, in May's work, power has many meanings and conceptual siblings, such as freedom and more. From the very beginning, children give raw expression to their muscular power and feel the deep need to be empowered by their caregivers. May uses a quotation from the American psychiatrist Harry Stack Sullivan to describe the early muscular assertion of the infant:

> The infant has as his mightiest tool the cry. The cry is a performance of the oral apparatus, the lips, mouth, throat, cheeks, vocal cords, intercostal muscles which man uses in the development of his security with his fellow man. I refer to language behavior, operations, including words. (quoted in May, 1972, p. 66)

To feel power is to feel significant. To be empowered is to "be able to *live out* that felt significance" (May, 1972, p. 37).

> Power is the birthright of every human being. It is the source of his self-esteem and the root of his conviction that he is interpersonally significant. . . . [It is] the inward conviction of significance, the individual's psychological and spiritual valuing by himself and by his fellows. (May, 1972, p. 243)

To experience one's own power is to experience the felt sense or belief that one counts, that one matters. Power, then, refers "to a person's conviction that he counts for something, that he has an effect on others, and that he can get recognition from his fellows" (May, 1972, p. 100).

Children seem to be born with the power motivation. It is like a "life force"—"an innate tendency to grow and master life" (quoted in May, 1972, p. 123). Thereafter, "the child needs all the aggressive [power] potential he can get to protect and assert his growing individuality" (May, 1972, p. 126). Self-affirmation, self-belief, self-esteem, and self-worth are all subsumed under the conceptual meaning of power. To have power is to have dignity. "The word *dignity,* coming from the Latin *dignus,* 'worthy', means a 'feeling of intrinsic worth'" (May, 1972, p. 138).

Power and Will

Power, for May, is related to will. Will refers to the ability to translate a bodily felt wish into concrete realization. Will bridges fantasy with reality, imagination with action, with actuality. Originally, especially between the ages of two to four, will expresses itself negatively, a phenomenon that has been alluded to in the beginning of the chapter. Through no-saying, young children are asserting their emerging and intensifying will. This is "a constructive expression of the power to be" (May, 1972, p. 143). They are attempting to appropriate power by asserting their newly emerging sense of self against benign opposition. To feel their existence, to stand out, they need to stand against or take an oppositional stance. Judicious parents understand this need on the part of their children, and they try to accommodate them, within limits and without allowing their children to violate the rights of others in the process. Through compromise, cooperation, cajoling, cowing, and firmly countering, judicious parents teach their children how to coordinate their will with the will of others. They enable their children to transform their negative willfulness into a positive force, into a strong healthy will.

Power and Innocence

In May's model of human development, the gradual expansion of the acquisition of power goes hand in hand with the increasing assumption of responsibility. "Responsibility . . . [is] commensurate with the power" (May, 1972, p. 244). Moreover, as children become increasingly more self-consciously aware of their own badness (evilishness) and the influence of their bad behavior on others, they begin to lose their naïve innocence. More power equals more capacity for good and evil equals more responsibility equals less innocence. Good parents assume their parenting role responsibly and expect increasingly more responsibilities from their children as they accord them more powers proportional to their stage of developmental maturity. As May views it, becoming mature involves awareness of one's powers, one's capacity for good and evil, and being perpetually vigilant at "achieving good not apart from evil but *in spite* of it" (May, 1972, p. 260). Growing up means the loss of innocence. Clinging or holding on to innocence signals a flaw in character development. Letting go of childhood innocence ushers in the natural movement toward growth and maturity. When children blame their misdeeds on imaginary friends, they are signaling their relative readiness to undergo a transition from innocence to responsibility assumption. From hereon, they will be suspended between their inclinations toward goodness and badness, "in an endless dialectic between good and evil" (May, 1972, p. 202). Responsible parents will not allow their growing children to eschew their responsibilities by taking refuge in their pseudoinnocence. It is also the height of irresponsibility for parents to view the irresponsible act of their children through pseudoinnocent eyes. These parents have never outgrown the naïve innocence of their own childhoods. Such naïve innocence is a defense against making constructive use of their own powers. Innocence that has not been transformed through repeated confrontation with the evilish side of oneself and life turns into destructiveness. "Innocence that cannot include the daimonic becomes evil" (May, 1972, p. 50). The renunciation of power leaves children and their parents unanchored in the world. For example, when parents renounce their power, their children, in the absence of a limiting structure, grow up feeling groundless. They may frighten themselves by the freedom for which they are not prepared. They may manipulate their parents for their own purposes without taking into account the long-term consequences of their intentions for themselves or others. They may fill the void created by their parents by engaging in risk-taking behavior that can be self-destructive or destructive of others. Innocence disallows openness to and learning from experience. It prevents the cultivation of compassion toward others.

> Experience . . . tempers the self, deepens consciousness and awareness, purges and sharpens our sight . . . whereas innocence acts as a blinder and tends to keep us from growing, from new awareness, from identifying with the suffering of mankind as well as its joys (both being foreign to the innocent person). (May, 1972, p. 210)

Adolescents may avoid the anxiety that accompanies the responsibility involved in searching for a vocation and values to live by, regressing to the carefree innocence of childhood. Judicious parents may perceive this as a temporary phase. Through gentle but firm guidance, they shepherd their children through this transitional phase. They have already prepared their children to be seduced by the natural pull of growth and maturity with its accompanying responsibility. Overly protective parents, naively innocent themselves, may succumb to the wish of the adolescent children to return to the womb.

Power and Communication

May connects power with the capacity for (preverbal, nonverbal, or verbal) communication. "Power is required for communication" (May, 1972, p. 245). From the beginning, infants communicate with their caregivers on a bodily level. The potency of crying in infants has already been touched on. Infants communicate with gestures, such as smiling or grimacing, and with their whole bodies. Parents, too, communicate with their infants even before they are born. May attributes importance to this image, which links tender communication to a symbiotic state of "we-ness" between mother and child (fetus). For May, optimal connectedness (union) equals optimal communication; failure in connectedness (disconnectedness) equals failure in communication (miscommunication). Communication in the context of connectedness is empowering to both participants or parties— parents and children. Moreover, when the intimate bond between parents and children is powerful and empowering, it can resiliently withstand instances of miscommunication. The strength of the bond of intimacy allows for quick repairs to failures in communication and for creative resolutions to communicative conflicts. The quality and tenor of communication will not be permitted to deteriorate to the point of threatening the bond of intimacy. "Violence and communication are mutually exclusive" (May, 1972, p. 65).

Words and gestures have the power to bring parents and children together or tear them apart. Our linguistic and communicative styles reveal our characters. We are how we speak and communicate with one another. Good parents communicate differently with one another and with their children than bad parents. The German existential philosopher Martin Heidegger refers to language as "the house of being" or, put differently, as the home where our core being dwells. Through language, parents communicate to their children not only the pragmatics of living but, more importantly, who they are and how they see their children as being and becoming. We are our emoting, gesturing, speaking bodies and more.

Inauthentic or vulgar language results in distancing, distrust, and destructiveness. May quotes Plato's Socrates: "The misuse of language is "harmful to the soul" (May, 1972, p. 67). He also quotes W. H. Auden as saying, "When it's [language] corrupted, people lose faith in what they hear, and this leads to violence" (May, 1972, p. 65). When parents use abusive language they violate the original integrative power of language. Their vulgar language takes on a disintegrative power. Originally, language serves the purpose of integration, of pulling the speaking participants toward one another. Language is symbolic—the meaning of the word "symbol," which is derived from the Greek, is "draw together" (May, 1972, p. 67). Authentic communication aims at communal inclusion and integration.

> [Authentic communication is] conciliatory and restorative . . . [It] overcomes the impulse to violence . . . [Authentic] communication makes community, and community is the possibility of human beings living together for their mutual psychological, physical, and spiritual nourishment . . . [Authentic] communication leads to community—that is, to understanding, intimacy and . . . mutual valuing. (May, 1972, pp. 246–47)

Families are children's original organic communities. Here we need to be flexible as to what constitutes families and not restrict their meaning to the traditional understanding of the term "family." A single parent and a child can a beautiful family make. Good parents hold as sacred the communal nature of the family. They are unifiers. They have reverence for the whole of which they are a part. Their everyday language reflects essentially and graciously this reverence. Their loving language, which is naturally reciprocated by their children, strengthens the unifying bond between them, empowers them, gives them a sense of belongingness and makes them feel more at home in the world.

May calls the subjective experience of integrative empowerment significance. It can therefore be deduced that the subjective experience of coercive or exploitative power is insignificance. Children who are exploited verbally are rendered powerless. Ironically, powerless children, in order to feel significant, identify with their tormentors and thus exploit those who are vulnerable relative to them in comparison. Powerless children may even invite exploitation in order to experience significance or seek revenge in passive-aggressive ways, such as the ways of academic negligence, procrastination, forgetfulness, and later, the ways of alcohol, cigarettes, and drugs. May holds that harboring feelings of powerlessness can later erupt into violent behavior.

May believes that the absence of constructive communication leads to pathology. He describes lack of communicativeness as "the inability to participate in the feeling and thoughts of others or to share oneself with others" (May, 1981, p. 21). Such a pathological parental communicativeness diminishes the intrinsic worth of children, constricts their consciousness, and enfeebles their coping power. It makes children significantly less likely to feel empowered and relatively free to stretch and expand the boundaries and confines of their destiny, which May defines as "the pattern of limits and talents that constitutes the 'givens' in life" (May, 1981, p. 89). Generally, faulty communicativeness begets in children the basic sense that deep inside they are at fault (self-hatred) and that there is a fault line in the world that feels unhomelike and unwelcoming.

It has already been briefly touched on that children blindly adopt maladaptive strategies in an effort to counter their feelings of powerlessness and insignificance. Like their larger versions, human adults, children prefer to be something rather than nothing, even if that means inviting others to further demean and devalue them through not only verbal but also physical violence. Whereas a feeling of generalized pleasure (May calls it "low-intensity feeling of ecstasy") accompanies integrative empowerment, a feeling of perverse pleasure ("high-intensity feeling of ecstasy"), along with fear, dread, and other emotions may accompany physical or verbal violence that follow acts of significance seeking. Bullied children "miss" their ritualistic encounters when their bullies fail to appear. Bullies themselves, like their "chosen" victims, become addicted to these high-intensity encounters. Some professional boxers similarly recall such encounters from their childhoods. Likewise, physically and/or verbally abusive husbands replicate the dramatic scripts of their own childhoods with their "chosen" spouses in a frantic effort to ward off feelings of worthlessness and powerlessness and simultaneously achieve a fleeting sense of pseudoempowerment and pseudosignificance. In a familial atmosphere where communicative empowerment is lacking, significance-seeking maladaptive strategies will abound. What in everyday life we label as "attention seeking" may be nothing more than significance seeking. The strategy may be as seemingly minor irritants as clinging, crying, and chronic complaining; or it may be as major as antisocial behavior, depression, or an eating disorder. Like adults, depressed children feel helpless (powerless) and thus hopeless. Instead of feeling enabled, they feel disabled. Instead of feeling empowered, they feel depleted and disempowered. Instead of seeing themselves as players, they perceive themselves as pawns. Instead of pursuing promising possibilities, they are frozen by their perceived impossibilities. To empower is to enable and to make possible; to disempower is to disable and to make impossible. Paradoxically, however, depressed children are focused on themselves. From this magnified self-pitying inward focus, they perversely derive a sense of pseudosignificance. This is reinforced, of course, by the attention that depression receives from "significant" others, such as parents and siblings. Similarly, adolescents with eating disorders become exaggeratedly focused on their bodily selves and their eating habits. Their consciousness is constricted; their horizons are narrowed; their worlds shrink. Feeling out of control (powerless), they seek control (distorted power) over their bodies, only to feel out of control (powerless). Their thinness signals their lack of substantial significance in the world. Yet, paradoxically, it triggers attention and concern. It simultaneously threatens with the disintegrative power of self-destruction and the exploitative power of destroying significant others. In the short story "The Chinese Lobster," which appears in a collection of short stories entitled *The Matisse Stories,* A. S. Byatt (1996) describes one of the main characters, an anorexic female college woman, as desperate, confused, suicidal, vengeful, and lacking imagination. She is seeking significance and a false sense of power through anorexic self-destructiveness, but also through her so-called artwork. In her so-called feminist thesis project she aims to critically deconstruct (destroy) Matisse's so-called sexist artwork through writing and artwork. Part of her artwork involves randomly throwing food and fecal matter at a Matisse reproduction. She then falsely accuses her thesis advisor of "sexual harassment." He in turn describes her to the Dean of Women, to whom she has submitted an official complaint, as not being able to work productively, as not having any talent, and as not being able to see. This is a fascinating description of the world of the eating-disordered person. The anorexic not only distorts her perception of her body, she simultaneously distorts what she sees and hears. Her interpretation of the world is distorted. She fails to "see" other possible meanings of Matisse's artwork, of her professor's interpretations. Her power of meaning making is compromised. The range of meanings that she sees are constricted. Powerlessness and disintegrative powerfulness place blinders on her perception. The implications are far reaching. The inability to see and the failure of imagination make it extremely difficult, if not impossible, for the person to empathize with and take the perspective of others. This brings us back to May's assertion that communication is connected with power. Distorted power equals distorted communication. To dramatize by way of an imaginative script between an anorexic and her parent: Through self-starvation, the anorexic is threatening, as Byatt puts it, to cease to exist, to cease to be. Obliquely and in a distorted fashion she is telling her parent: "I'll kill myself if you do not accept me as I am." However, this is never explicitly communicated to the parent. The parent is devastated, unnerved, and enraged by the daughter's refusal to eat, a task on which the parent is focused. Indirectly and in a twisted manner, the parent is saying to the daughter: "I will not love you unless you conduct yourself the way I want you to." This is a paradigmatic illustration of indirect (inauthentic) communication between parent and child. Authentic communicativeness requires the ability on the part of parents and their children to participate in the feeling and thoughts of one another and the ability to share themselves with each other.

Power and Passion

Children are thrust into existence with the life impulse to *exist*—to stand out, to take a stand, to emerge, to grow, and to become. They are born with the power to be and become themselves. When this power of being and becoming is frustrated, it turns on itself and is transformed into distorted forms of power. In fact, one way of looking at what kind of adult characters children will become is to look at how they went about finding and using their powers. Adult personalities reflect the vicissitudes of power acquisition in childhood. Granted that there are biological, economic, political, sociohistorical, and cultural factors that exert critical influences on the degree to which children are allowed and encouraged in discovering and appropriating their emerging powers. The focus of the present project is simply on the existential meaning of optimal and faulty parenting.

In May's view, power and passion are inextricably interrelated. Passion (eros) energizes and permeates power. Passion refers to a deep desire to seek union with not only others, but also with one's potentialities, with higher forms of beauty, goodness, and truth. The meaning of passion also includes the urge to create, to make meaningful forms out of that which is formless, and the urge to procreate and perpetuate oneself into the future. It is also the urge to grow, to become whole and a part of a larger whole, to move toward self-transcendence. It further contains the urge to learn, to know, and to probe the mysteries of life. It is the impulse to affirm life, living, and that which is most alive. It is ecstatically saying an emphatic Yes! to life.

Children are born with this passion and exuberance for life. Parents whose own passion for living has not been suppressed resonate to this mirrored impulse. Parents and children enliven each other. They bring out the liveliest selves in one another. The dance of life comes into being in the synchrony of the passions. In this precious encounter is found one of life's supreme joys. This mutual affirmation of the passions of life is empowering for both children and parents.

Good parents not only resonate to and affirm but also constructively channel their children's passions. This they do through their attuned responsiveness; through provision of proper and feasible experiences and opportunities for the positive direction of their children's passions. Normal, healthy infants and children will display delight as their potentialities are transformed into empowering competencies. They derive pleasure—in spite of repeated frustrations and pain-producing failures—from attempting, exercising, and mastering abilities such as crawling, walking, running, and jumping. Other examples of pleasure-eliciting acquired capacities are: babbling, speaking, reading, writing, singing, playing, and dancing. The learning of new and exciting activities is unlimited. "There is both nature and nurture in every step of this actualization . . . [of their] potentialities" (May, 1972, p. 122). Parents, who are "good enough," are attuned to their children's potentialities and, through their guidance, encouragement, and timely interventions, make it possible for their children to actualize these potentials.

The process of becoming aware of attempting to actualize potentialities is not only pleasure producing but also anxiety producing. This anxiety has multiple sources. It involves a fusion of fears such as fear of failure, fear of pain, fear of the unknown. The fusion of fears converge into producing an amorphous feeling of anxiety. This anxiety is further compounded by the fact that the emergence of potentialities and the attempt at their actualization are not always met with affirming responsiveness. Parents and other authoritative representatives of the culture, being concerned, place limitations on and may urge delay in the actualization of some of these potentialities. For example, "the potentiality for sexual intercourse, which takes a decisive leap ahead at puberty, brings excitement and joy but also the anxiety associated with new relationships and new responsibilities" (May, 1972, p. 122). During early adolescence, the genital potentialities of young adolescents are transformed into actual powers. They become capable of parenting babies. Parents, in our particular culture, typically are not ready to welcome the immediate actualization of such a potentiality. Rather, parents are usually inclined to be concerned and to caution their teenage children against premature parenthood. This can become a source of anxiety-producing conflict between parents and their adolescent children. However, creative solutions are possible when these conflicts are constructively confronted. Properly guided, early adolescents can find outlets for their sexual urges in creative activities such as art, dance, and music, or in sports.

In May's dialectical model of human development, where there is a yes (to life), there is also a no (to life). In others words, there exists in human existence a positive life force (*eros*) and a negative life force (*daimon*). In May's view, the relationship between the two life forces is not a simple one. "The diamonic . . . is part of eros" (May, 1969, p. 163); "the daimonic . . . overlaps with eros, that is some of eros is daimonic . . . not . . . all eros is" (May in Reeves, 1977, p. 306). Daimon is a diabolical force. The term "diabolic," "comes from the Greek *dia* plus *ballein* and means to 'tear apart, to confuse, to throw into discord'" (May, 1985, p. 157). The daimonic mode of being "refers to any capacity which has the *power* to push the individual into *disintegrative* behavior" (May in Reeves, 1977, p. 305; emphasis added). The course of human life unfolds in a spiraling dialectical movement between integrative and disintegrative powerful passions, partly absorbing and partly being absorbed into each other resulting in different levels of integration or disintegration. Children (and adults) tear existing models apart and put together something new, creative, and original. In this instance, disintegrative power is put (absorbed) into the service of integrative power. In Charles Dickens's (2001) *Great Expectations,* the character of one of the main protagonists, Estella, is bent and broken, but only to reform into a better shape.[2] In his youth, Adolf Hitler is depicted as an aspiring mediocre artist. Regardless of his level of talent, he is struggling to give expression to the creative force within himself. In adulthood, it is abundantly clear that Hitler's creative urge is absorbed into and overtaken by the destructive urge within. Disintegrative power can, therefore, be absorbed into integrative power or it can deteriorate into destructive and exploitative power. These powers are equivalent to forces of good and evil, within and without. May views human beings as having the power to be both good and evil. They also have the capacity to recognize the good as well as the evil within and outside of themselves. They have the power to pause and choose to cultivate the goodness within.

Parents are their children's heroes. Good parents serve as good models and bad parents serve as bad models for their children. Consciously or unconsciously, children absorb their parents' propensities toward good and evil into the core of their beings. Given a modicum of (even inconsistent) care, children identify with their parents' ways. Children learn important lessons from parents who remain calm in explosive situations; from parents who are able to contain their temper; from parents who are able to bracket their worries and level of fatigue in order to empathetically listen to their children's concerns. Children learn how to be from observing their parents' ways of being with them, with each other, and with others in general. The line of demarcation between children's (and adults') leanings toward being good and being bad is thin. It is very easy to slip into being bad. It is much harder to cultivate the capacity to avoid and resist such slippage. The capacity to resist being bad can be nurtured through modeling and educational training. The power to be good can triumph over the power to be bad. Granted this is an ideal portrait. Nevertheless, given our human limitations and failings, it is something to strive for. Good parents empower their children to resist their evilish proclivities. Exploitative parenting disempowers children and renders them powerless to confront the temptation to be bad; it predisposes them to be exploited or to become exploiters themselves. Although destined in this direction, May holds that the destination can, within limits (though with difficulty), be reversed, for humans can always confront their destinies and break generational repetitions. There is always a margin of choice and a degree of freedom.

Growing up or maturing means becoming sensitive to and accepting our increased potentiality for both good and evil. It means becoming increasingly aware of our own power. It means owning up to our positive as well as our negative passions. It means forever being vigilant, for our integrity (integration) lies in the delicate balance between our power to be good and our power to be bad. It is out of this (creative) tension between our capacities for good and evil that our individuality or personhood is created. This creation simultaneously mirrors our human universality.

Good is that which empowers and affirms the existential worth of the other as well as the self; evil is that which disempowers and denies the existential worth of the other as well as the self. Good parents empower and validate the worth of their children; bad parents disempower and repeatedly and relentlessly violate the worth of their children. The ratio of good to bad parenting boomerangs on the parents: Good parents are empowered; bad parents are disempowered. Good and evil are not all-or-nothing phenomena. There are degrees of good and evil. There is always a leeway for "refining" the level of our goodness as parents and as human beings.

As May sees it, just as humans are mixtures of love and hate, they are simultaneously fusions of good and evil. We are bestowed with the blessings and the burdens of the powers to pause, to be self-aware, to reflect on ourselves, to be conscientiously self-conscious (and thus called to listen to the call of conscience), to make choices and take actions, and to be responsible for the consequences of our actions. These powers demand from us to muster the courage to confront our destinies and to look into ourselves and become aware of, acknowledge, and own our proclivities toward good as well as evil.

Escape from evil is simultaneously escape from our destiny, freedom, and responsibility. It is equivalent to the surrender of those powers which humanize us. The assumption of innocence and the denial of evil are themselves evilish stances. Such stances not only diminish us as human beings, they also can lead to destruction and violence.

Parents who view themselves and their children and families (and whatever they subsume under "we," "us," and "our") as innocent and good on the one hand, and whoever belongs to the "they" as bad and evilish, are creating dichotomies which will make it very difficult for their children to grow up feeling compassionate and whole. That which is bad and evil within themselves and their children will not remain quiescent. The repression of evil will exact a high human price. Instances of damaging and projective mean accusations, insensitivities, and unexpected violent eruptions can all be manifestations of the denial of evil.

Power and Love

Love and power are intertwined. Integrative power enables us to love. "[O]ne must have power within oneself to be able to love" (May, 1972, p. 114). Mature love, in turn, is the source of what May calls "nutrient power," the capacity to care for the welfare and the growth of others. Love and power are not simply emotions and impulses; they are "states of being or processes," which overlap and require each other.

> Love needs power if it is to be more than sentimentality and power needs love if it is not to slide into manipulation.

Without tenderness, the caring and the sensitivity for the feelings and delight of the other is absent; and without self-assertion the capacity to put one's self into the act [of loving] is missing. When love and power are seen as opposites, "love" tends to be the abject surrender of one [person] . . . and the subtle (or not so subtle) domination of the other. (May, 1972, pp. 115, 250)

Will and power are naturally related. In everyday discourse, reference is made to "will-power." From May's perspective, the linkage is intuitively correct, but the meaning attributed to these two hyphenated terms is a distortion of experiential reality. Contrary to the claims of "will-power" proponents, we cannot "will" ourselves to sleep, to succeed overnight, to stop overeating, overdrinking, or smoking, to get rid of our symptomatic behaviors and diseases, and to attain instant gratification and everlasting happiness. May defines will as "the capacity to organize one's self so that movement in a certain direction or toward a certain goal may take place" (May, 1969, p. 218). Will here refers to the concrete actualization of the potential power for self-assertion. It is to be recalled that when this self-assertion first develops, it manifests itself negatively in children's opposition to their parents and other authority figures. Injudicious parents who interpret this negatively are likely to stultify their children's emerging self-assertion. As a consequence, children learn to dissociate their will from the love of their parents, which they previously enjoyed. Their powers of willing and loving are compromised.

May asserts that love and will need to remain united. Care unites love and will. Caring parents, who interpret their children's original self-assertion positively, enable their children to maintain the union between their own empowering love and their children's emerging powers of willing and loving. Love and will "are not united by automatic biological growth but must be part of our conscious development" (May, 1969, p. 283). It must also be part of our preconscious and unconscious development, which is a by-product of our averaged internalized loving and hateful transactions with our significant others.

For May, care is the source of love and will. As figures, love and will originate from the ground of care. In the light of, relatively speaking, consistent parental care, infants experience a preverbal, bodily affirmation of life. Developmentally, this preverbal yes is the source of our first freedom; the verbal no is the source of our second freedom, according to May. It is, however, care that provides the nutrient which nurtures the flowering of the two freedoms. It is care that makes it possible for love to grow. It is in this sense that care precedes and integrates love and will.

Paradoxically, care is not only the source of love, but becomes an important dimension of love. Because the optimal development and growth of our children is contingent on the integration of love and power (will), it is necessary to understand what May means by the concept of love. May provides us with descriptions of forms or kinds of love: sexual love, erotic love (which aims at creation or procreation through the establishment of a lasting union with an other), philial love (which aims at establishing a nonsexual intimate friendship with an other), and "agapic" love (which seeks a spiritual union with an unconditionally accepting other). Integrated love is a fusion or a selective blending ("gestalting") of these forms of love. The key descriptors of integrated love, in the light of May's writings, are: acceptance, affirmation, altruism, care, concern, delight, (compassionate) disinterest, enjoyment, esteem, forgiveness, identification (with the other's joys and sorrows), mercy, passion, presence, recognition, relaxation, respect, responsibility, self-abnegation, tenderness, and unconditionality. Love, therefore, is a process which requires endless effort and creative courage. Courage is the ability to move forward in spite of life's setbacks. It is the capacity to be fully committed in spite of life's unpredictability. Creative courage is the openness for new forms or relational patterns to emerge in spite of the allure of the familiar. It is this creatively courageous effort that integratively empowers our children and indirectly ourselves which we call love. It is love that makes us reject the allure of exploitative power given our temporary and tenuous absolute authority over our vulnerable children.

Just as love and power go together, so too are lovelessness (or suffocating, sentimental or overprotective love) and powerlessness (or exploitative power) interrelated.

Neurotic power (or magic) is in direct proportion to the early powerlessness. (May, 1972, p. 131)

Compassion—the capacity to have passion with another—implies empathy, the ability to see the world as the other person sees it. (May, 1972, p. 230)

Assertion, affirmation of the self, and even aggression at times are not only unavoidable but healthy in the developing love relationship. (May, 1972, p. 118)

[The meaning of the term aggression in this context is linked to its derivation from the] Latin root *aggredi*, which means to go forward, to approach. (May, 1972, p. 150)

When a person has not been loved or has been loved inconsistently by a mother or a father who was [her or] himself radically insecure, there develops in his later aggression a penchant for revenge on the world, a need to destroy the world for others in as much as it was good for him. (May, 1972, p. 159)

[A person may resort to violence] to prove one's power, to establish the worth of the self. (May, 1972, p. 187)

When parents fail to love their children properly, they communicate to them the essential message that they do not care for or about them. "Care is a state in which something [or someone] does *matter*" (May, 1969, p. 289). When they are inconsistently loved, children acquire a deep ambivalence about their essential worth. Moreover, when parents' love for their children is suffocatingly sentimental and overly protective, they implant in their children a lasting sense of helplessness and powerlessness.

Exploitative power and powerlessness are two sides of the same coin. They grow out of the same soil of lovelessness (or improper, exploitative love). Children who are properly loved experience within the core of their being that they matter; that they are irreplaceable, precious, special, and unique in the eyes of their parents. From this they derive a basic feeling of at-homeness in the world, a feeling of belonging. Through being authentically loved, children acquire the capacity to love—to be compassionate and empathic. Unloved or improperly loved children feel either that they do not matter or they feel deeply ambivalent about their worth as persons. Feeling powerless or neurotically powerful, they lack a secure sense of having a place in the world. Deep inside they feel that they do not belong; that they are not at home in the world. Lacking compassion, they easily become cruel and antisocial. In the absence of integrative love and power, their consciousness becomes constricted, their horizons narrow, their judgments faulty, their choices unwise and their actions irresponsible.

Power and Courage

The concept of courage has already been alluded to briefly. It has been defined in that context as the ability to move forward in spite of the presence of barriers, obstacles, frustrations, and failures. Children are born with an original native courage. In the face of repeated failures, feelings of fear and uncertainty, and in the face of the unknown, children, unceasingly, seek new challenges in order to acquire a sense of mastery and competence. These are empowering experiences. Thus, the modalities of being powerful (experiencing themselves as having a critical role in the acquisition of their own competencies and a significant influence on their world) and being courageous feed on and bolster one another.

Courage, for May, is a strength that is required for the acquisition of all other strengths. It is the virtue behind all other virtues. It is a central concept in May's writings. Early in his career, May is influenced by the works of the theologian and philosopher Paul Tillich and the psychologist and psychotherapist Alfred Adler, both of whom stressed the importance of courage for optimal development and self-actualization. Tillich (1952) has written a book entitled *The Courage to Be,* and May (1975) has later written *The Courage to Create.* The Adlerians (Dreikurs, 1964) repeatedly emphasize the link between courage and encouragement and the importance of the "courage to be imperfect." In order to build on their original courage, children need to be encouraged. Parental encouragement results in children's empowerment. Parental discouragement leads to children's disempowerment, to feelings of powerlessness. Children are discouraged by parental humiliation and overprotection. Discouraged children compensate for their powerlessness by using maladaptive strategies in order to at least attain a pseudosense of power and a pseudosense of place in their discouraging melieu. Parents thus need not only to encourage, but to avoid discouraging their children. They have to allow their children to discover their own strengths and limitations. They must acknowledge the courage behind children's attempts at such discoveries. Children need to feel free to try and fail without being humiliated or protectively prevented from trying again. They have the right to fail without losing their sense of personal value. Psychologists, again and again, point to the importance of the separation of the action from the actor. Parents are advised to disapprove of the misdeed, but not to undermine the personal integrity of the doer. Parents, especially perfectionistic parents, need to guard against disallowing their children from cultivating "the courage to be imperfect," which has to be emphatically affirmed. Just like adults, being human, children are imperfect. Similarly, they are bound to make mistakes, from which they may or may not immediately learn. As parents, we do not want our children to become afraid of making mistakes. Debilitating fear is the enemy of courage. Courage means forging ahead in the face of fear. But the pull to press on in spite of fear is in the service of expansion, growth, wholeness, significance, integration, and integrity, and not for the purpose of irresponsible and reckless disregard for self and others. Fearlessness is therefore not equivalent to courage. The fearless lack good judgment. Courageous efforts on the part of children need to be reinforced. Those that, in retrospect, prove to have been mistaken can be viewed as vehicles for learning or simply a reflection of our human frailty and folly, which could be faced, if fitting, from a comical perspective. The spirit that ought to pervade after the mistake has been made is that of moving on, not dispirited, but with renewed vigor.

Originally, courage is physical; later, it develops into different kinds of courage: cognitive, psychological, social, moral, spiritual, and existential. May traces the growth of courage to early parent-child relations:

> The [nourishing] source of this physical courage appears to lie originally in the relationship between the infant and its mother [or father], specifically his trust in his solidarity with her [or him] and, consequently, with the world. Physical cowardice, on the other hand, seems to come from an early rejection, an early feeling that the mother [or father] will not support her [or his] child and may even turn against him in his fright; so that henceforth every effort the youngster makes, he makes on his own. Such a person finds it inconceivable that others would support him. (May, 1972, p.176)

Children's preverbal or bodily trust in their solidarity with their parents is the soil out of which courage is cultivated. From this vital sense of solidarity, children are empowered to take a stand or stand up against even their own parents in acts of self-assertion. From this basic feeling of at-oneness with their parents, children acquire the courage to be and become themselves. Children can move forward, make choices, and take action on their own when they carry with them the assuring presence of that sense of solidarity that they have with their parents. This feeling of communion is the source of their autonomy and freedom. Children who lack this fundamental feeling of connectedness with their parents feel less anchored in the world. They are likely to be either more cowardly or, in compensation, more reckless. They are more prone to experiencing feelings of abandonment, loneliness, and vulnerability. Nourished by a sense of solidarity, children learn to stand firm, or take a firm stand, without becoming unyieldingly stubborn. Their tenaciousness is grounded in a sense of stability and security. Their solidity is sound. Their steadfastness has been described by some psychologists as a kind of "hardiness." Secured by a basic faith in themselves, they confront the fearsome with hope and resilience. Anchored in solidarity, their solid sense of self persists in spite of the tension-producing trials and tribulations of everyday living. They remain centered despite the threat of decentering experiences. This is what May means by courage: "[A]ll living beings . . . require . . . centeredness . . . *every existing person has the character of self-affirmation, the need to preserve his [or her] centeredness.* The particular name we give this self-affirmation in human beings is 'courage'" (May, 1983, p. 27).

6
Parenting and the Life of the Spirit

The concept of courage occupies a special place in the works of Gelven and May.[1] The convergence in the meaning they both make of the concept of courage is fascinating. Then again, it should come of no surprise, for both have an existential orientation. The range of the meaning of courage expands richly in the thought of Gelven, for it comes to signify and disclose ultimate truths about ourselves as human beings.

Courage, for Gelven, refers to the affirmation and appropriation of our own significance.

> [C]ourage is the acceptance or the embracing of our own *worth*. To be courageous, then, is to recognize that we do *matter*, that we have worth simply in being who we are, and that whatever actions we might take deserve to follow from the bold *confrontation* of our own being. . . . [T]o be cowardly is to shrink, to become small; it is ultimately to be eclipsed; it is not to matter. Shame is loss of significance, a surrender of one's importance and *belonging*. (Gelven, 1990, p. 196; emphasis added)

This mattering, for Gelven, is simultaneously a source of celebration and burdensome responsibility. "[T]o be courageous is to confront the worth of one's own existence, to accept the burden and the honor that who one is matters, that it is important to be" (Gelven, 1990, p. 197). Moreover, "unless it matters who we are—which is what courage celebrates—nothing else can matter either" (Gelven, 1998, p. 65). We thus need to celebrate and be responsible for who we are becoming.

By being born, according to Gelven, infants become members of the human species. The act of birth is a gift which bestows on them existential worth. They are entitled to be treated as worthy simply for coming into existence. Their joining of the human community is a cause for celebration. The sacred rituals of birthday celebrations and the care and deliberation taken in naming infants are not fortuitous events.

> The etymology of the term [celebrate], from the Latin *celeber*, meaning "frequented" or "populous," suggests the communal nature of celebration; it is a gathering together of the people to honor or to esteem someone or an

event of importance for the group. Strictly, then, one cannot celebrate alone. And this is why the celebration of birthdays is so fitting, for the feted one is accepted into the fold, as it were; the rejoicing is because the child is *ours,* as the famous line from Handel's *Messiah* sings, "Unto *us* a son [or daughter] is *given.*" (Gelven, 1991, p. 81)

For Gelven, these celebratory rituals are spiritually laden acts of graciousness that signify the welcoming of the newcomers into their human home. Their purpose is to affirm children's primordial need for communal belonging. Out of this originary belonging emerges the promise of becoming: what infants promise to become. Children come "into existence burdened and favored with [fate and] fortune at . . . [their] *birth*" (Gelven, 1991, p. 79). "To celebrate . . . [their] birth is therefore to celebrate . . . [their] fate or fortune, but also to celebrate . . . [their] independence of them" (Gelven, 1991, pp. 79–80). Their fate and fortune are not only what they inherit physically, psychologically, materially, culturally and spiritually, but also what they do with them. "Birth begins not only a new link in the chain but also a possibility of responsibility and guilt" (Gelven, 1991, p. 80). Children will contribute to the shaping of their own character by their responsible and irresponsible acts. Nevertheless, parents of newly born infants, under average expectant circumstances, look upon the future becoming of their children with hope and promise. In the anticipation and observation of the unfolding of their children's lives, parents confront the essential meaning of their own existence.

Not all parents welcome the arrival of their newly born infants in the same manner or to the same degree. "Celebration can be a success or a failure. We are celebrating beings, but this does not mean that all celebrations are equally well done. Indeed one can fail at celebrating altogether. . . . Celebration can also be denied altogether" (Gelven, 1991, p. 81). If celebration signifies the affirmation of the existential worth and communal belonging of children, then the absence of celebration may signal the denial of such welcome. Psychologists have observed infants in orphanages, whose basic physical needs were met, become listless, lose their appetite for living, and die. Young infants, throughout the world, are abandoned and abused. Female infanticide is still practiced in certain parts of the human globe. Infants and children, who are very vulnerable to their parents' whims, can also be used as targets of displaced frustration, manipulation, and projection. Under these and other similarly demeaning circumstances, children feel unwelcome, unworthy, and not at home in the world. Lacking existential worth and a sense of communal belonging, these children's natural movement toward becoming their true selves is either arrested or retarded.

Our children belong to us, just as we belong to them, not in the possessive sense, but rather in the sense of those who belong because they love each other. It is in the spirit of this sacred belonging that we as parents are more than willing to make sacrifices for the sake of our children, for the sake of that which is greater than ourselves. To use Gelven's terms, we sacrifice that which is "dear" for that which is "precious." We sacrifice that which will gratify us personally in order to protect and prepare that which we treasure, for an optimally envisioned future. In the process, we are ennobled by our sacrificial offerings and sufferings. This is, in part, what being good parents means. Becoming good parents entails learning to sacrifice and suffer nobly. Goodness equals nobility. By learning to become good parents, we are learning to become good human beings and vice versa. This does not mean, Gelven reminds us, that good parents cannot feel resentment toward those parents who are unwilling to sacrifice what is dear for the sake of what is precious. This form of resentment is not allowed, however, to deteriorate into self-pity or hatred of humanity.

Mattering, for being and the birth of being, and belonging have spiritual significance for Gelven. They are necessary for our spirituality. They are necessary for the maintenance and nourishment of our souls. This is why the proper response to the birth of a new life, a child, is welcoming, a celebration, gift giving, and gratitude. Being grateful and generously giving are essential modes of being spiritual. The welcoming celebration of shared belonging is a spiritual ritual. We resonate to the Biblical story of the prodigal son because of the father's welcoming celebration of shared belonging. The son has returned home to where he belongs. The father welcomes the almost lost son with open arms and celebrates his coming home with humbled gratitude and generous giving to the chagrin and envy of the loyal brother who does not understand the spiritual significance of this momentously moving reunion. In the father's eyes, his son matters more than his son's wrongful prodigality. Mattering triumphs over justice. The father's act of celebratory welcoming signifies forgiveness. The father forgives the son's guilt because he values more the son's existential worth. In this act of generosity, the father's own existential worth is unknowingly expanded. The father is willing to absorb the prodigal son's wrongdoing (injustice), which the loyal brother is unwilling to accept, for the sake of affirming something greater, their shared belonging. To forgive, for Gelven, is of the essence of what it means to be a good and courageous parent. In good parenting, mercy (forgiveness) triumphs over justice.

There is goodness and joy in mattering and belonging. When children (and adults) feel that they matter and belong, they feel more real. Consequently, for Gelven, spirituality, of which belonging and mattering are manifestations, is not merely a subjective matter. Being spiritual is also objective in the sense that it makes us feel more real. Children (and adults) who do not feel that they matter and that they belong, therefore, feel less real, less substantial, less solid and less grounded. Lacking solidarity, they search for solidity in the wrong places and through the wrong means, such as buying solid possessions in order to feel more real; or becoming preoccupied with appearances and the impact of impressions on others; or by becoming promiscuously sexual; or through smoking, drinking, and drug taking in order to numb present reality or escape into alternate realities.

Mattering and belonging require constant cultivation. The threats of alienation, estrangement, and devaluation of worth are present possibilities. Children (and adults) are always vulnerable to succumbing to such threats. It requires courage to affirm, again and again, the mattering and belonging of ourselves and others. It takes ceaselessly courageous effort on the part of parents to create a sacred space for children in which they feel at home in the world. It is the sacred duty of parents to generate a dwelling place where children feel they truly belong.

> [T]he essence of a home is that which makes belonging possible . . . loving parents, like poets refining language or painters refining the wedding of color and form, refine the welcome of belonging in a myriad of ways, from the kindly but stern discipline of parental authority to the reverence shown the institutional structure, the spontaneous grasp of youthful folly and the balanced need for comfort and scolding, even down to the well-laid fire, the smell of cooking, the privacy extended to each child, the cheerful listening to the clumsy telling of the schoolboy's misadventures, and the unfathomed trust that assures us we remain welcome even when we go astray. These, too, are refinements, as fine they show us . . . what a home truly means. (Gelven, 1996, p. 27)

Our children are our greatest gifts They are unique, irreplaceable, and precious. "[P]reciousness . . . is found in the realization that who [they] . . . are matters independently of [their] behavior" (Gelven, 1998, p. 72). "[W]e love our children simply because they are ours even if they are bad. . . . Even as adults our worth is not reducible to our moral rectitude, else we could neither forgive or be forgiven" (Gelven, 1998, p. 72). Our children belong because they matter; they matter because they belong. They matter for being and belonging, not only to us but also to something greater than ourselves, before which we stand, or kneel, in wonder and awe, gratitude and reverence.

As good parents, we need to treat our children as being worthwhile. We ought to treat them as if they matter, "even if such treatment may seem undeserved by the appearance of unruly behavior" (Gelven, 1996, pp. 70–71). Our children will come to feel that they are important, that they make a difference, that they deserve respect, that they are esteemed and that they have intrinsic significance. In the light of such respectful treatment, the intrinsic worth of both children and parents are united. Such a union reinforces their mutual sense of belonging. Only after experiencing existential worth can our children achieve autonomous moral goodness. What psychologists today call "self-esteem" is grounded in what we have been calling existential mattering and belonging.

Gelven's grounding of courage in belonging parallels May's anchoring of courage in solidarity. For Gelven, however, this sense of belonging, as we have discovered, has a spiritual significance that May's sense of solidarity does not. Moreover, both Gelven and May view courage as the ability to confront the essential modalities and polarities of existence, such as freedom and destiny (fate). Gelven delves deeper into this existential confrontation.

Courage is the ability to engage life's challenges and problems, stresses and storms, in spite of our fears, weaknesses, and imperfections, without losing our existential worth. Courage, for Gelven, requires the following attributes: concentration, discipline, endurance, patience, sacrifice, steadfastness, truthfulness, and unashamedness. Courage, which is a form of moral strength, also requires a correct appreciation of things, good judgment, awareness of just causes and of what is important in life, and perception of the good.

Gelven mines deeper into the meaning of courage. In his excavation into the meaning of courage, he comes upon the insight that, in its most essential existential meaning, courage is: (1) the ability "to endure the tension between the opposing forces of attraction and repulsion. . . . [W]hat repels is the fear of pain, what attracts is the lure of significance and wholeness" (Gelven, 1990, p. 198). In other words, in our confrontation of the polarities of existence, we experience tension. To be courageous is to endure the tension. Moreover, Gelven contends that as human beings we are naturally truth seekers. "[I]f we are denied knowledge and certainty, yet at the same time obligated to confront the truth [about ourselves], then courage is a logical necessity" (Gelven, 1990, p. 200). In its first meaning then, courage is *necessary* for confronting the opposing dimensions of our lives that can potentially reveal truths about our existential reality. (2) In its second interrelated essential meaning, "*courage* [is understood] *as a mode of truth*" (Gelven, 1990, p. 202). Although their surface meanings may seem dissimilar, in their deepest meanings, courage and truth move toward convergence.

> [T]ruth is vacuous without courage. It is precisely because we already know that the two terms, truth and courage, are different that it is possible to define them in such boldly similar ways. In courage we confront our meaning; in truth we confront reality as the unfolding of meaning, and a part of our being in truth is the courageous enduring of our fate. . . . [T]o confront . . . means to come face to face with that from which we would turn away but cannot. We are, in confrontation, both attracted and repelled, drawn to and drawn away from. . . . Truth is a confrontation because the unfolding of reality burdens us with fate and guilt, that is, acceptance [of fate] and acknowledgment [of guilt]. At the same time it attracts us with both pleasure and beauty, that is, affirmation [of pleasure] and submission [to beauty]. (Gelven, 1990, p. 198)

It is courageous to accept my fate. It is courageous to acknowledge my guilt. But it is also courageous to affirm what I am, in the rejoicing of pleasure, and to yield to what is revealed in the submission to its beauty. So the fourfold structure of confrontation reveals the meaning of courage.

Yet, courage is also necessary for a home to matter, for a tribunal to weigh my worth, for my story to unfold with the dread inevitability of my fate. And it is courageous to yield to the allure of the unfolding beauty that is the

world as my desire. So courage is found to lie in the very unfolding of truth.
(Gelven, 1990, p. 203)

Being courageous, ultimately, is being in truth. "To be true to truth," existential truth, the truth about ourselves, is the call to be courageous. Courage requires (is) truth; truth requires (is) courage. Being and becoming who we are in truth require courage. Courage is at the heart of the unfolding of our being and becoming. To be and become a person is to be courageous. "[P]ersons . . . *are* persons because of the [courageous] struggle with [the forces of] good and evil" (Gelven, 1998, p. 152). We are fundamentally conflictive beings. We are suspended and tensed between "pro-person" and "anti-person" forces. Being and becoming persons necessitate the constant struggle and, on the whole, triumph over the anti-person forces.

> [T]he pro-person force consists in all those attributes that transcend the inevitable: forgiveness, generosity, bestowal, grace, beauty, nobility and laughter. . . . It is far more powerful to forgive than to offend, to bestow with graciousness than to yield to imperatives, to be gracious than demanding, to love than to hate, to laugh than to denounce, to celebrate beauty than to fear its distraction. It is not merely nicer and more pleasant, it is more powerful; it demands greater strength and reveals greater truths. . . . This [is the] realization of the power of being a person. . . . [L]ove is a curious warrior. . . . [B]eing gentle is not soft but hard. . . . [T]hese personalist weapons [can be viewed] as offensive rather than defensive. (Gelven, 1998, p. 146)

It is easier to give in to anti-person forces; it is harder to marshal the pro-person forces. It is simpler to be cowardly than courageous. It is more effortless to be pulled down by the "deceit" ridden spirit of ignobility ("from pettiness, meanness . . . to inelegance, vulgarity and insensitivity") than to be pulled up by the honorable and worthy spirit of nobility (Galven, 1998, p. 131). The "quest" to be and become persons is a spiritual lifelong project which requires a courageous movement toward being and living in truth in the face of all the anti-person forces from within and from without, We are journeying selves who are potential participants in *The Quest for the Fine* (Gelven, 1996). This pursuit of perfection (existential and moral excellence), not perfectionism, is a holy endeavor. The process of becoming fine involves vigilance and hard work the short aim of which is the attainment of small improvements and refinements. This human, all too human, life story contains innumerable slip-ups, internal and external temptations, failures, calamities, inherited and acquired limitations, and other environmental and historical forces all of which threaten to diminish us as persons. Moreover, as Gelven reminds us, we are forever suspended between the polarities of existence. We are tensed between our fate and freedom. We can accept or reject our fate. We can make use of our limited freedom or deny it. We are suspended between our existential guilt, over our failures at personhood, and our capacity to forgive ourselves and others. We can either acknowledge or refute our existential guilt. We can forgive and thus affirm the worth of personhood or refuse to go beyond the wrongful act. We are poised between experiencing the pleasures and joys that our home world offers us, on the one hand, and experiencing pain and suffering on the other hand. We can affirm or deny our pleasures and joys. We can react with self-pity or act out in rage in response to our pain and suffering; or we can endure our pain and suffering with nobility. We are suspended between that which is beautiful, not in the superficial sense of appearances on the surface, and that which is obscene and vulgar. We can either submit to that which is beautiful in the deep and truth-revealing sense or we can distractedly gloss over or disdain it. We can also either resist or give in to obscenity and vulgarity.

When negative emotions rise and tempers flare, it is so easy to slide into vulgarity in our interactions with our children. The possibility for repair and redemption is almost always there, but it is the pattern and repetition that count. Over time we are diminished by obscenity and vulgarity. Our lives consequently become typified by wretchedness. The tenor and quality of our lives can be gauged by the ratio of the beautiful to the ugly. It is also measured by the degree in which we are able to transform the ugly into the beautiful. The allure of the paintings of Paul Klee and Henri Matisse lies, in a great part, in their creative capacities to transform that which is ordinarily ugly into a beautiful work of art. Similarly, our life is like a work of art which requires the ability to change the ugly into the beautiful. Tender hugging and kissing carry with them the authoritative truth of beauty. For Gelven, beauty equals truth equals nobility. In one sense, that which is beautiful is that which is loved. In the beauty of loving, we, along with our children, learn about ourselves. We discover new dimensions (truths) about ourselves. In the light of a beautiful interpersonal experience, we become united in surrendering to something greater than ourselves. Our ritualistic demonstrations of love become *ours;* yet, at the same time they signify something deeper and more universal than ourselves.

As parents, it is our sacred duty, taking into account the limitations of our capacities and resources, to expose our children to beautiful artifacts, objects, and surroundings, natural and human-made. These are beautiful embodiments of human excellence. Beautiful paintings, musical compositions, poetry, prose, and architecture are a few examples. In Byatt's short story "The Chinese Lobster," one of the three collected *Matisse Stories,* the art professor makes the assertion that in the presence of a beautiful painting, such as a Matisse painting, he comes close to experiencing the sacred. The proper response to such an experience, he adds, is to fall on our knees in worshipful gratitude. What has been unveiled to him is that experiencing such "pleasure" is a source of "power" and that is "life" itself—what life is about; what makes life meaningful for him. It discloses to him one of the faces of truth, the truth about life, an existential truth. His graduate student, however, has nothing but disdain for Matisse. She is untalented, cannot "see," and does not work (which he perceives as a form of violence). She is filled with self-contempt and contempt for Matisse and his paintings. Gelven informs us that self-hate is a form of evil. It stands in the way of openness and learning. One needs to have self-respect and love oneself in order to love learning. Lacking an existential sense of worth, the graduate student is unable to learn. Instead, she slides into disdainful distortion, despair, vulgarity, and the threat of violence against the self.

Experiences that allow us to near the sacred elevate our souls and enhance our existential worth. If the art professor can near the sacred at the art museum, the parent can near the sacred at home. When we look at our children in the proper way, *life makes sense.* We matter. We belong. Life is sacred. The sacred is that which makes our "ultimate belonging" possible. The sacred is present in the triumph of pro-person forces over the anti-person forces. For instance, in the polarity of fate versus freedom, the anti-person stance is to deny freedom and to accept the *inevitability* of fate. The pro-person stance is: "We cannot deny the inevitable, but we can find its limits. The limit to the inevitable must be the sacred; the forfeiture of these limits is evil" (Gelven, 1998, p. 128). When parents (adult individuals) perceive reality as nothing other than necessity, it drives out all possibilities of generous giving, graciousness, and gratitude. Such parents no longer place themselves in the proper position of selfless self-preservation and sacrifice. Fine parents, while accepting their as well as their children's fates, try to stretch the boundaries of their own and encourage their children to expand their destinies. Those parents who reject or refuse to confront their fates may find themselves repeating unhealthy generational patterns of living.

Parents who easily forget their failures at parenting, and thus their proper guilt, are likely to repeat their mistakes. The reference here is to "real guilt" and not to "neurotic guilt"—guilt that is either imagined or out of proportion to the misdeed that triggered it. Forgetters or refuters of existential guilt are likely to slide precipitously into the muddy ground of immoral, wicked, and ultimately evil conduct, where parents no longer care or notice the effect of their harmful conduct on their children. Parents who genuinely acknowledge their guilt and consequently atone, learn, and change from such acknowledgment are likely to forgive themselves, be forgiven, and thus to enhance their existential worth. It is proper guilt which grounds our mattering and moral worth. Without such existential guilt, authentic selfhood is not possible. Without the possibility of existential failure, failing at existence, the striving toward existential success or moral excellence would not be an alternative possibility. Good parents graciously forgive their children because they have reverence for the preciousness of their children as persons, which overrides that which their children have done. Children also observe and learn from how forgiving their parents are toward family members, relatives, friends, acquaintances, and strangers.

Children also observe how affirming their parents are of the pleasures and joys of life and living. Do they derive pleasure from what they see, hear, smell, taste and touch, literally and metaphorically? Are their joyous passions aroused by what the world has to offer them? Do they share their pleasures and joys with them? Are they grateful for the pleasure- and joy-eliciting bestowals? How do their parents respond to the pain-and-suffering-producing bestowals of life? Parents who endure their pain and suffering nobly are imparting an important lesson in courage to their children. How do their parents react to agonizing experiences of failure? Gelven instructs us that, as persons, we can succeed at failure. Just as in suffering, we can endure defeat nobly. "Defeat endured," Gelven tells us, is "defeat defeated." There is beauty in suffering nobly, he adds. It is an expression of the struggle toward moral perfection. It allows sufferers to hold on to the meaningfulness of life.

Parents (and educators) need to cultivate the instincts of children toward caring for the true, the good, and the beautiful. Parents are called on to provide their children with metaphorical mirrors through which children can discover and learn about themselves. Stories, poems, paintings, musical melodies and songs, and countless other sounds and sights, beautiful and sometimes not so beautiful, can serve as metaphorical mirrors. This kind of learning may bring pleasure as well as pain to children as they embrace the truth about themselves and about life. We cannot totally shield our children from vulgarity, ugliness, obscenity, and evil. Moreover, these anti-person proclivities are also within them and within us. We need to demonstrate, by way of example, how we can courageously triumph over these anti-person forces and guide them in this common human struggle. Similarly, we can introduce them to other exemplars, past or present, fictional or real, who struggled and triumphed over vulgarity within and without. There is beauty and nobility in overcoming such anti-person forces.

There is beauty and grace in the way refined parents show respect for their children. For the most part, they approach their parenting duty acceptingly and joyously. It is an understatement to say that in their meeting of their parental responsibilities, they go above and beyond the call of duty. They view parenting as a sacred and spiritual vocation. They treat their children as unique, precious, and irreplaceable. In their graciousness, their existential worth is united with the existential worth of their children. They repeatedly affirm their shared belonging with their children. Overall, they succeed in creating a dwelling space where their children feel relaxed, playful, and free to be and become themselves. In this home, there is love, laughter, and learning. Humor here makes the members of the family united and whole. This kind of humor, Gelven describes as an "inverted" form of love. The graciousness of the parents (and refined persons in general) is manifested in "gentility in language and demeanor, etiquette, politeness, [nonpossessive] generosity and compassion" (Gelven, 1996, p. 68). As parents, we owe it to our children to embody and live out these "external manifestations of grace." The training in the practice of such social virtues will in time contribute to the refinement of our children's character. Such refined behavior originates from a deep respect for oneself and for others. These "'good manners' . . . [are] grounded in respect and made beautiful by grace" (Gelven, 1996, p. 68). Just as we lovingly worship our children, our children worship us.

> Fine parents realize they may become objects of hero worship to their children, yet they dare not tell these precious learners all their own private faults lest they scandalize. . . . [H]eroes must be all the more heroic in their flawed humanity as they inspire their admirers, for the cracks in the idol do not disbar idolatry. . . . [T]he fine are acutely aware that they themselves radiate what is greater than themselves. . . . Conscious of themselves as radiating welcome, the fine heroically accept the burden and need of mastery, even though they are aware of their own finitude and imperfection. . . . The fine are always themselves sources of refinement, as fine teachers [or parents] not only instruct, but embody learning. . . . [F]ine teachers [or parents] become mentors of the superior students [or children] but cannot disburden themselves of the roles that must be played. (Gelven, 1996, p. 123)

Gelven says that the pathos of goodness is joy. In other words, being good makes us feel the passion of joy. This does not mean, however, that the good are always joyous. In fact, from a Gelvenian viewpoint, there is no joy without pain and suffering. There are inevitable painful parts to the parenting process. But as parents we endure these painful parts for the sake of our beloved children. Presently, our children may make us miserable. Circumstances disallow us from always experiencing joy with our children. It is goodness, though, not the circumstances, which makes us experience joy. We can always nostalgically remember or hopefully anticipate a joyous past or future with our children.

All things being relatively normal, we gratefully accept the gift that has been bestowed upon us: our children. This feeling of gratitude accompanies our seemingly unearned passion of joy. This passion of joy lifts us outward and upward beyond ourselves and enables us to experience a feeling of communion with something larger than ourselves before which we stand, or kneel in piety with a sense of wonder or awe. It is as if a transcendent power has bestowed upon us an undeserved gift.

The triumph of our ecstatic sense of union with and belonging to our children, and they with us, while at the same time letting them go and become their own persons *over* the present and potential discord, alienation, grasping attachment, or premature letting go without proper protection and preparation, is the source of our joy in being good parents. There is no accord without discord. Conflict, doubt, and struggle are harsh realities that precede the experience of joy. The passion of joy infuses the vocation of parenting with the sense of the sacred.

In his conclusion to *Critique of Practical Reason*, the German philosopher Immanuel Kant (1956) writes, "Two things fill the mind with ever new and increasing admiration and awe, the oftener and more steadily we reflect on them:

the starry heavens above me and the moral law within me" (p. 166).[2] In a commentary on this quotation, Lewis White Beck (1960) writes, "That the two [things] were deeply connected in Kant's own life of feeling, no doubt having first been joined by Kant's mother, is sufficiently attested by the early biographers who knew him" (p. 282). Kant seems to have revered his pious mother. "He speaks of her as having 'planted and nourished the seed of the good' and 'opened [his] heart to the impressions of nature,' the same combination as in the present apothegm" (p. 282). In a further wonderfully illuminating reflection and refinement on Kant's apothegm, Gelven (2000) writes,

> What he [Kant] does not specifically say—though perhaps as the supreme synthesizer , he should—is that we cannot have the one without the other. For it is only because of my own unique moral integrity that the starry heavens can amaze; and it is only because of a vastness that outreaches my grasp that this moral integrity—the uniqueness of my "soul"—becomes awesome. (p. 79)

What Gelven is saying here is that as we refine our moral integrity, our perception of the world is correlatively refined. As we refine our character, we look at and relate to the world differently. Becoming good persons is becoming good parents. The reverse is also true. To conclude with a variation on Kant's apothegm: Two things fill our mindful heart with ever-deepening admiration, wonder, and joy: our capacity for love and goodness from within and the beautiful unfolding of the goodness of our loved and loving children from without.

In her book *Silas Marner*, George Eliot (pseudonym of Mary Ann [or Marian] Evans) weaves a story about a miserly weaver, whose sole purpose in life is the accumulation of money. Silas the weaver maintains his distance from the people of Raveloe, a village near which he has settled. The citizens of Raveloe tolerate his abnormality because of the usefulness of his trade to the region.

Silas Marner's transformation occurs when he loses his savings to theft and is bestowed by destiny a very young child to raise as his adopted daughter.

> [T]his child . . . stirred fibers that had never been moved in Raveloe—old quiverings of tenderness—old impressions of awe at the presentiment of some Power presiding over his life; for his imagination had not yet extricated itself from the sense of mystery in the child's presence. (Eliot, 1966, p. 152)

While gazing in the calm eyes of his child Eppie, Silas feels "a certain awe . . .such as we feel before some quiet majesty or beauty in the earth or sky" (p. 161). As she grows, she creates "fresh links between his life and the lives from which he had hitherto shrunk continually into narrower isolation" (p. 171). And as he attends and responds to her developing and changing needs and desires, he is forced to focus on something other than himself. Because of her natural love of "sunshine, and living sounds, and living movements" he feels more connected to nature.

Eppie made her father Silas "look for images of that time in the ties and charities that bound together the families of his neighbours" (pp. 170–71). She reawakened "his senses with her fresh life . . . warming him into joy because *she* had joy" (p. 172). And "as her life unfolded, his soul, long stupefied in a cold narrow prison, was unfolding too, and trembling gradually into full consciousness" (p. 173).

As he experiences the trials and tribulations of parenting, Silas proves to be a caring, tender, kind, and attentive father. In spite of experiencing "the incompatible demands of love" (p. 173), Silas maintains his tolerant and gentle attitude toward his daughter. When he is advised to use punishment to discipline his child for her propensity toward mischief, he decides against it. "If she makes me a bit o' trouble," he reasons, "I can bear it, And she's got no tricks but what she'll grow out of" (p. 177). The intensity of his attentiveness is mirrored in how he listens to his daughter: "[W]hen Eppie's talking o' things, I see nothing but what she's a-saying" (p. 186).

"By seeking what was needful for Eppie, by sharing the effect that everything produced on her," Silas experiences a transformation in his faith and "a consciousness of unity between his past and present" (p. 191). Eppie "had come to link him once more with the whole world" (p. 179). "Perfect love," which Eliot describes as a "breath of poetry," had surrounded Eppie (p. 196). In the home that Silas created, there was a "sense of presiding goodness and the human trust which come with all pure peace and joy" (p. 191). "The love between him and the child blent them into one, and there was a love between the child and the world" (p. 179). Silas reflects, "[s]ince the time the child was sent to me and I've come to love her as myself, I've had light enough to trusten by" (p. 196).

In passing, Eliot gives us, her readers, a wonderfully inspiring moral to the story:

> In the old days there were angels who came and took men by the hand and led them away from the city of destruction. We see no white-winged angels now. But yet men are led away from threatening destruction; a hand is put into theirs, which leads them forth gently towards a calm and bright land, so that they look no more backward; and the hand may be a little child's. (p. 180)

Appendix
The Story of *To Kill a Mockingbird* Revisited

Harper Lee's *To Kill a Mockingbird* (Lee, 1960), hereafter referred to as *TKM,* is fundamentally a moral novel.[1] The drama takes place in Maycomb, a small town in southern Alabama. The time is the great depression. The story begins to unfold in 1933, but the focus of the dramatic action is the year 1935. Although recovery is around the corner,

> there was nowhere to go, nothing to buy it with, nothing to see outside the boundaries of Maycomb County. But it was a time of vague optimism for some of the people. Maycomb County has recently been told that it had *nothing to fear but fear itself.* (*TKM,* pp. 5–6; emphasis added)

This incidental inclusion of President Franklin Roosevelt's proclamation that the only thing to fear is fear itself, which is nothing short of a moral exhortation, sets up a central thematic preoccupation of this novel. The theme of fear, of dark forces within and without, and how people live with it, are undermined by it, or able to overcome it, is at the heart of the unfolding narrative. Without fear, there can neither be courage nor cowardice. Without courage, there is no goodness; without cowardice, there is no evil.

TKM is more than a simplistic depiction of an almost deadly conflict between good, as exemplified by the courageous Atticus Finch, and evil, as embodied by the cowardly Bob Ewell. It is about how hard it is to sustain one's goodness in the face of our precious vulnerability to the internal as well as the external forces of evil. This vulnerability is the primordial source of fear. The depression has made the people of Maycomb acutely aware of their vulnerability and, thus, afraid. Fear is in the air everywhere. This uneasy mode of being is redirected by the majority of the citizens of Maycomb County into a concrete fear of that which is different: different in race, class, sex, and even age. In a fascinatingly revealing aside, a minor character, Mr. Avery, a neighbor who lives on the same street on which the Finch family resides, blames the Finch children for the unexpected change in weather: " 'See what you've done?' he said. 'Hasn't snowed in Maycomb since Appomattox. It's bad children like you makes the seasons change' " (*TKM,* p.65). In this instance, Mr. Avery is not dealing nobly and courageously with his fear of the unknown. Yet, it is the same Mr. Avery who puts his life on the line in his attempt to save the furniture of a neighbor's house that is almost consumed by fire. Here he is able to bravely override his fear for the sake of a noble cause. It is easier to be cowardly and wicked than it is to be courageous and good.

Above all, *TKM* is about how a good father, Atticus Finch, imparts his goodness to his children, "Scout" (Jean Louise) and "Jem" (Jeremy Atticus). Again and again, Scout and Jem observe their father's courage in action. They witness, firsthand, the way he confronts the ugly and evilish pressures and threats while maintaining his dignified and principled stance. They absorb the passionate contagion of his noble suffering. In being appointed by Judge John Taylor to defend Tom Robinson, a black man falsely accused by Bob Ewell of raping his daughter, Mayella, Atticus Finch has been made utterly vulnerable, given the place and time, and thus is fearful, least of all for himself and most for all for his children. Because he aims to give Tom Robinson the best defense he can muster, he has aroused the raving ire of the majority of Maycombians. He knows that as a consequence of all this, his children will be subjected to ugly talk and confrontations, a concern which turns into an actuality. Here is his younger brother, Jack, asking him about how bad it is going to get:

> "It couldn't be worse, Jack." . . . "You know what's going to happen as well as I do, Jack, and I hope and pray I can get Jem and Scout through it without bitterness, and most of all, without catching Maycomb's usual disease. Why reasonable people go stark raving mad when anything involving a Negro comes up, is something I don't pretend to understand. . . . I just hope that Jem and Scout come to me for their answers instead of listening to the town. I hope they trust me enough . . . Jean Louise"?
>
> My scalp jumped. I stuck my head around the corner. "Sir?"
>
> "Go to bed."
>
> I scurried to my room and went to bed. . . . I never figured out how Atticus knew I was listening, and it was not until many years later that I realized he wanted me to hear every word he said. (*TKM*, pp. 88–89)

As can be seen from the quotation above, the story is narrated from the double perspective of a child, Scout, who is six, seven, and eight years old during the span of the novel, and as an adult looking retrospectively on her childhood. For the most part, the unfolding of the story is anchored in the spontaneous observations, recollections, and reflections of, primarily, Scout and her brother Jem, who is four years older than his sister and, secondarily, those of their friend "Dill" (Charles Baker Harris), who is about one year older than Scout. Their father, Atticus Finch, is a single, middle-aged parent nearing fifty, who practices law, and serves as a state legislator, a post to which he has been elected and reelected. He is a widower whose wife died when Scout was two years of age. He is assisted in raising of the children by Calpurnia, a black housekeeper, whom Atticus considers as a member of the family and later, as the date of the critical trial approaches, by his sister Alexandra, who turns out to be diametrically opposed to her brother in character and ideology.

> [A]fter getting Uncle Jack started [in the practice of medicine by investing in his brother's education], Atticus derived a reasonable income from the law. He liked Maycomb, he was Maycomb County born and bred; he knew his people, they knew him, and because of [his ancestor] Simon Finch's industry, Atticus was related by blood or marriage to nearly every family in town. (*TKM,* p. 5)

Divided somewhat loosely into two parts, with eleven sections in the first part and twenty sections in the second part, the narrative, in *TKM,* contains significant episodes in the children's lives as described from the narrator's point of view. There is a wonderful movement between the seemingly faithful description of events as they are occurring and the apparently spontaneous reflections on these events. This back-and-forth movement is so smooth and captivating that the reader is uncertain, at times, whether these reflective observations are those of Scout the precocious child or Scout the young adult reflecting back on her childhood. Regardless, these episodes describe what it was like to grow up as a child in the fictional home of Atticus Finch and in the fictional town of Maycomb, in Maycomb County, Alabama, between the years 1933 and 1935.

The major episodes, stories within the larger story, which will hereafter be described, in this evaluative summary, are those that shine light on how a father, Atticus Finch, imports goodness and moral strength to his children, Scout and Jem.

The Going-to-School Episode. Scout's first day in school is deeply disheartening and disappointing. Miss Caroline Fisher, her first-grade teacher, who is new to the school and the region for she comes from North Alabama, is not appreciative of Scout's ability to read and write for it purportedly will obfuscate her plan to introduce a new method of teaching into the classroom. She thus advises Scout to tell her father not to teach her anymore. That is the end of it and there is no need for further dialogue about it. The relationship between Scout and Miss Caroline is further soured when Scout attempts to mediate on behalf of her classmates to explain the ways of Maycombians, which Miss Caroline doesn't seem to comprehend, and thus is a source of misunderstanding between herself and the students. Instead of valuing Scout's effort at mediation, Miss Caroline attempts to punish Scout for her audacious intervention.

Here is what transpires at home that evening between father and daughter:

> After supper, Atticus sat down with the paper and called, "Scout, ready to read?" The Lord sent me more than I could bear, and I went to the front porch. Atticus followed me.
> "Something wrong, Scout?"

I told Atticus I didn't feel very well and didn't think I'd go to school any more if it was all right with him.

Atticus sat down in the swing and crossed his legs. His fingers wandered to his watch pocket; he said that was the only way he could think. He waited in amiable silence . . .

Bit by bit, I told him the day's misfortunes. "—and she said you taught me all wrong, so we can't read any more, ever. Please don't send me back, please sir." (*TKM*, p. 29)

After listening thoughtfully to his daughter, Atticus tells his daughter that she would understand and get along with others if she considered things from their point of view. He encourages her to climb into Miss Caroline's skin and walk around in it. "We could not expect her to learn all Maycomb's ways in one day, and we could not hold her responsible when she knew no better" (*TKM*, p. 30). And after standing firm on the matter of going to school, he concludes in this manner:

"Do you know what a compromise is?" he asked.
"Bending the law?"
"No, an agreement reached by mutual concessions. It works this way," he said.
"If you'll concede the necessity of going to school, well go on reading every night just as we always have. Is it a bargain?"
"Yes sir."
"We'll consider it sealed without the usual formality," Atticus said, when he saw me preparing to spit.
As I opened the front screen door Atticus said, "By the way, Scout, you'd better not say anything at school about our agreement."
"Why not?"
"I'm afraid our activities would be received with considerable disapprobation by the more learned authorities."
Jem and I were accustomed to our father's last-will-and-testament diction and we were at all times free to interrupt Atticus for a translation when it was beyond our understanding.
"Huh, sir?"
"I never went to school [Atticus was home schooled]," he said, "but I have a feeling that if you tell Miss Caroline we read every night she'll get after me, and I wouldn't want her after *me*." (*TKM*, pp. 31–32).

In this episode, Scout encounters a teacher who is different in terms of her regional background. When Miss Caroline first introduces herself, the "class murmured apprehensively should she prove to harbor her share of the peculiarities indigenous to that region" (*TKM*, p. 16):

(When Alabama seceded from the Union on January 11, 1861, Winston County [North Alabama] seceded from Alabama, and every child in Maycomb County knew it.) North Alabama was full of Liquor Interests, Big Mules, steel companies, Republicans, professors and other persons of no background. (*TKM*, p. 16)

Scout is frustrated, angered, and hurt by her teacher's inability to understand her (the Maycombian) point of view. She is apprehensive about returning to school only to collide again with her new inhospitable teacher who has also forbidden her to read with her father, a sacred ritual that binds father and daughter. After sensing her dispirited state, Atticus listens to her respectfully and empathetically. He encourages her to take the viewpoint of her teacher and strikes a compromise with her, with which she wholeheartedly concurs: They will continue with the ritual and she will continue to go to school. Throughout, Atticus is calm, comforting, and composed. In the light of this tender transaction, important learnings are taking place. She is learning about the true meaning of compromise, while maintaining her sense of worth. She is learning about the importance of looking at things from another person's perspective. She is learning about how important it is to bracket one's judgment, reach out and be inclusive of the different other who is essentially another human like oneself. Above all, the relationship between father and daughter, in a small and imperceptible way, is strengthened and deepened.

The Boo-Radley-as-the-Frightfully-Fascinating-Other Episode. Arthur "Boo" Radley is a reclusive neighbor who fascinates the three children. They are simultaneously attracted and repelled by his phantom presence. As constructed in their imagination, they fear his existence. They attempt to confront their fears by constructing and enacting playful dramas about his life and by seeking unsuccessful contact with him. An overriding element of risk and bravery characterizes their efforts at finding out what Boo looked like. Atticus has a dual response to his intermittent awareness of their activities. On the one hand, he implicitly understands their childish fascination with that which cannot be seen and is there, given the neighborhood and town talk about his eccentricities; he also realizes that all children go through such a phase of adventuresome attraction to such activities. On the other hand, he disapproves of their "asinine game," which contains elements of making fun of a life of a human being; he also objects strongly to their infringement on the personal privacy of Boo Radley.

How would we [the children] like it [Atticus says to them] if Atticus barged in on us without knocking, when we were in our rooms at night? We were, in effect, doing the same thing to Mr. Radley. What Mr. Radley did might seem peculiar to us, but it did not seem peculiar to him. Furthermore, had it not occurred to us that the civil way to communicate with another being was by the front door instead of a side window. Lastly, we were to stay away from that house until we were invited there. (*TKM*, p. 49)

Atticus is dimly aware that along with children's naïve innocence, there is an accompanying predisposition toward cruelty and insensitivity. Patiently, and at times impatiently, he tries to goad them toward civility and social responsibility. Interestingly, as the episode unravels, the children, especially Jem, are beginning to realize that the monstrous other on whom they have projected their evilish tendencies is not only a real human being, but also a caring, good-hearted and gift-giving soul. Moreover, throughout the episode, the children are learning how to exercise their physical courage in the face of their fears. They are also slowly learning a critical lesson: It may take physical bravery to unveil the secrets of a frightening mysterious other, but it is cowardly to violate the privacy and personhood of the other. It takes a different kind of courage to tolerate the tensions of one's own inner terror and not to succumb to the allure of displacing one's inner turmoil upon a vulnerable other. It takes a higher type of courage to transform one's naïve innocence into socially aware responsibility and refined civility.

The Snow-and-Fire Episodes. One morning, Scout "awoke, looked out of the window and nearly died of fright. My screams brought Atticus from his bathroom half-shaven. 'The *world's ending,* Atticus! Please do something—I dragged him to the window and pointed. 'No it's not,' he said. 'It's snowing'" (*TKM,* p. 64). The snow episode begins with the fear of snow and ends with the playful and joyous building of a snowman. At first Atticus is skeptical about the prospect of making a snowman, given that the snow is wet and lightly falling. But Jem builds an inside structure made of mud and an outside coating and embellishment of snow. Upon completing the project, with the help of Scout, the father is amazed and pleasantly surprised. The snowman turns out to be like a caricature of the neighbor, Mr. Richard Avery.

> Atticus said we had done a jim-dandy job. "I didn't know how you were going to do it," he said to Jem, "but from now on I'll never worry about what will become of you, son, you'll always have an idea."
>
> Jem's ear reddened from Atticus's compliment, but he looked up sharply when he saw Atticus stepping back. Atticus squinted at the snowman a while. He grinned, then laughed. "Son, I can't tell what you're going to be—an engineer, a lawyer or a portrait painter. You've perpetrated a near libel here in the front yard. We've got to disguise this fellow." (*TKM,* p. 67)

Atticus affirms Jem's competencies and talents, laughs at the accuracy of the caricature, but advises his son to alter the snowman so as not to offend Mr. Avery or make fun of him in the neighborhood.

Scout is gently awakened by her father in the early hours of the morning only to be told that their neighbor's house is on fire. Atticus instructs Jem to stand at a safe distance with and keep a watchful eye on his sister, while he along with other neighbors try first to put out the fire, and proving fruitless, attempt to save her furniture. In place of his father, Jem comforts his frightened sister:

Jem put his arm around me "Hush, Scout," he said. "It ain't time to worry yet. I'll let you know when." . . .

I saw Atticus carrying Miss Maudie's heavy oak rocker chair, and thought it sensible of him to save what she valued most.

. . . [Scout voices concern about the danger of fire spreading to her own house.]

"Don't worry, Scout, it ain't time to worry yet," said Jem. He pointed. "Looka yonder."

In a group of neighbors, Atticus was standing with his hands in his overcoat pockets. He might have been watching a football game. Miss Maudi was beside him.

"See there, he's not worried yet," said Jem. (*TKM*, pp. 69–70)

Jem, in assuaging the fear of his sister, uses the soothing phrases of his father. He also keeps an eye on his father as a point of reference to his own responses to the fire disaster. The father's distant and calm presence reduces the children's fears. Everything is still all right with the world.

The Uncle-Jack-Christmas-Visit Episode. During a ritualistic Christmas dinner visit at Aunt Alexandra's home in nearby Finch's Landing, Scout gets into a fist fight with her cousin Francis. She punches and calls her cousin a "whore lady" because he defames her daddy and calls him a "nigger lover." Upon hearing Francis's side of the story, Uncle Jack punishes Scout by spanking her. After abruptly returning home, Scout is hurt and enraged by her visiting uncle's actions. And she tells him so. After retreating to her room, her uncle follows her to explain to her his disappointment in her conduct. She counters:

"You ain't fair," I said, "you ain't fair."

Uncle Jack's eyebrows went up. "Not fair? How not?"

"You're real nice, Uncle Jack, an' I reckon I love you even after what you did, but you don't understand children much."

Uncle Jack put his hand on his hips and looked down at me. "And why do I not understand children, Miss Jean Louise? Such conduct as yours required little understanding. It was obstreperous, disorderly and abusive."

"You gonna give me a chance to tell you? I don't mean to sass you, I'm just trying to tell you."

Uncle Jack sat down on the bed. His eyebrows came together and he peered up at me from under them. "Proceed," he said.

I took a deep breath. "Well, in the first place you never stopped to gimme a chance to tell you my side of it—you just lit right into me. When Jem an' I fuss Atticus doesn't ever just listen to Jem's side of it, he hears mine too, an' in the second place you told me never to use words like that except in extreme provocation, and Francis provoked me enough to knock his block off." (*TKM*, pp. 85–86)

What this transaction between uncle and niece shows is that in the eyes of Scout, Atticus is perceived by his daughter as basically being fair and understanding of children.

The Shooting-of-the-Mad-Dog Episode. Because of the sedentary nature of his vocation and avocation, the middle-aged Atticus does not seem to be a man of action or special distinction of which the children can be publicly proud. "He did not do the things our schoolmates' fathers did: he never went hunting, he did not play poker or fish or drink or smoke. He sat in the livingroom and read" (*TKM*, p. 89). But a day comes when a mad dog strays into the Finch's residential street. All the residents are frightened and are behind closed doors. The sheriff of Maycomb County, Mr. Heck Tate, and Atticus are outside awaiting the nearing of the mad dog. Mr. Tate hands the rifle to Atticus. Atticus, reluctantly, takes the rifle and, expertly handling the gun as an extension of himself, shoots the dog dead. The children are watching the spectacle initially with fear and then with pride. Jem is struck dumb and is mesmerized. Mr. Tate addresses Jem: "Didn't you know your daddy's—" "Hush, Heck," said Atticus, "let's go back to town" (*TKM*, p. 97). The good neighbor, Miss Maudi Atkinson, later responds to Jem's bafflement as to why his father has never mentioned anything about his marksmanship:

> "If your father's anything, he's civilized in his heart. Marksmanship's a gift of God, a talent—oh, you have to practice to make it perfect, but shootin's different from playing the piano or the like. I think maybe he put his gun down when he realized that God had given him an unfair advantage over most living things. I guess he decided he wouldn't shoot till he had to, and he had to today."
>
> "Looks like he'd be proud of it," I [Scout] said.
>
> "People in their right minds never take pride in their talents," said Miss Maudi. (*TKM*, p. 98)

Jem begins to understand. It takes more courage to put down than to take up a gun. Scout still thinks that it may have slipped her father's mind to make mention of his sharpshooting skill. Jem responds,

> "Naw, Scout, it's something you wouldn't understand. Atticus is real old, but I wouldn't care if he couldn't do anything—I wouldn't care if he couldn't do a blessed thing."
>
> Jem picked up a rock and threw it jubilantly at the carhouse. Running after it, he called back: "Atticus is a *gentleman*, just like me!" (*TKM*, p. 99; emphasis added)

Jem comes to the eye-opening realization that it takes more courage to be a gentleman than a tough man, a person who displays and takes pride in his raw power.

The Encounter-with-the-Aged-Mrs.-Dubose Episode. Mrs. Henry Lafayette Dubose, a neighbor, is a very old, "cantankerous" woman who "disapproved heartily" of the doings of Atticus Finch and his children. Although confined to her bed and wheelchair, Mrs. Dubose is ruthless in her verbal attacks on the children. The children are unable to go to town without taking the risk of encountering her. Scout and Jem have come to fear and hate her. The children are repeatedly wounded by her accusatory comments and observations. When Jem complains to his father, Atticus responds, "Easy does it, son. . . . She's an old lady and she's ill. You just hold your head high and be a gentleman. Whatever she says to you, it's your job not to let her make you mad" (*TKM*, p. 100).

With his father's example, guidance, and support, Jem is able to hold his head high as a gentleman as he faces Mrs. Dubose's verbal bombardment. But one day after he turns twelve years of age, his "phase of self-conscious rectitude" is broken. Upon being subjected to a verbal assassination of his father's character by Mrs. Dubose, Jem returns a short while later to take revenge, while she is inside the house, by decapitating her camellia bushes. Upon learning of what has transpired, Atticus orders Jem to have a talk with Mrs. Dubose, who in turn demands that in compensation for his destruction Jem will have to read to her daily for about a month. Upon Atticus's strong urging, Jem reluctantly acquiesces. Accompanied by Scout, Jem begins to read daily to Mrs. Dubose. While unknown to the children, Mrs. Dubose is weaning herself from her morphine addiction. She is thus using Jem's reading as a distraction from the agonizing pain of withdrawal. Her verbal harassment, however, never ceases. "Thorough the weeks he [Jem] cultivated an expression of polite and detached interest, which he would present to her in answer to her most blood-curdling inventions" (*TKM*, p. 110).

Mrs. Dubose dies soon after. Before she dies, she sends Jem a candy box with a perfect Snow-on-the-Mountain camellia. Atticus explains that it is her way of telling Jem that "everything's all right now." He then explains to his son why he made him read to her:

> I wanted you to see something about her—I wanted you to see what real courage is, instead of getting the idea that courage is a man with a gun in his hand. It's when you know you're licked before you begin but you begin anyway and you see it through no matter what. You rarely win but sometimes you do. Mrs. Dubose won, all ninety-eight pounds of her. According to her views, she died beholden to nothing and nobody. She was the bravest person I ever knew. (*TKM*, p. 112)

In Atticus's eyes, Mrs. Dubose confronted her pain with courage. This courage sets her free from a state of addictive dependency. What Atticus does not mention is that although Mrs. Dubose demonstrates the meaning of courage in one domain, she, at the same time, shows a failure in courage in another domain: the manner of her treatment of the vulnerable children. Her being old and ill does not excuse her maltreatment of the children.

The episodes described above appear in Part One of *TKM;* those that appear below are delineated in Part Two.

The Going-to-Calpurnia's-Church Episode. While Atticus is away on legislative business in Montgomery, Calpurnia invites the children to come to church with her. She makes sure that they are clean and dressed impeccably for the special occasion. Calpurnia comments, "I don't want anybody sayin' I don't look after my children" (*TKM*, p. 118). What is most revealing about this episode is the children's natural openness and eagerness to attend an African American church service, seemingly being the only two white children to enter the First Purchase African M.E. Church. In spite of the unexpected objection of the "contentious" Miss Lula to bringing white children to a Negro church, Reverend Sykes and the rest of the congregation welcome the children with open arms. The experience turns out to be a great learning experience for Scout and Jem. Inspired by this adventure, Scout asks Calpurnia if she can come and visit her in her own home. Calpurnia tells her that she is glad to have her at any time. Again, what is in evidence here is, with Atticus's nurturing and moral training, the children's willingness to reach out and embrace that which is different, in spite of the bumps and bruises along the way.

The Aunt-Alexandra-Comes-to-Stay Episode. Whether it was at Atticus's invitation or due to her persuasive initiative, Aunt Alexandra comes to live with the Finch family, in anticipation of a "hot" summer. Aunt Alexandra is everything Atticus is not. She is opinionated and her opinions are entrenched in a rigid adherence to the importance of differences in heredity, class, race, sex, and age.

Aunt Alexandra sets herself the task of changing the ways of the Finch household. When Scout tells her father, within her Aunt's hearing range, about the trip to Calpurnia's church, Atticus seems to enjoy it. When she follows it by expressing her desire to visit Calpurnia's home, Aunt Alexandra intervenes and forbids it. And when Scout responds by saying that she did not ask her permission, Atticus intervenes firmly to remind Scout to mind what Aunt Alexandra tells her. Atticus finds himself in a delicate and conflictual situation. On the one hand, he does not want to undermine his sister's authority in the presence of the children; on the other hand, he does not want to stifle his children's free-spirited, yet responsible ways. Thus, when his sister asks him to firmly remind Scout and Jem to behave in ways that befit the Finches, he reluctantly agrees, but when he seriously approaches his children about the subject, he falters:

> "Your aunt has asked me . . . to tell you you must try to behave like the little lady and gentleman that you are . . . and to impress upon you . . . that you are not from run-of-the-mill people, that you are the product of several generations of gentle breeding." . . .
> Stunned, Jem and I looked at each other, then at Atticus, whose collar seemed to worry him . . .

For no reason I felt myself beginning to cry, but I could not stop. This was not my father. My father never thought these thoughts. My father never spoke so. . . . Through my tears I saw Jem standing in a similar pool of isolation, his head cocked to one side.

There was nowhere to go, but I turned to go and met Atticus's vest front. I buried my head in it. . . .

"Atticus, is all this behavin' an' stuff gonna make things different? I mean are you . . . ?"

I felt his hand on the back of my head. "Don't you worry about anything," he said. "It's not time to worry."

When I heard that, I knew he had come back to us. . . .

"You really want us to do all that? I can't remember everything Finches are supposed to do. . . ."

"I don't want you to remember it. Forget it."

He went to the door and out of the room, shutting the door behind him. He nearly slammed it, but caught himself at the last minute and closed it softly. (*TKM*, pp. 133–34)

He follows the soft shutting of the door by peeking right back in and humoring himself by comparing himself to his cousin who ended up in a mental asylum: "Get more like Cousin Joshua every day, don't I?" (*TKM*, p. 134).

From this brief interaction with their father, Scout and Jem are appropriating a great deal from the goodness of this exceptional man. Caught between two loyalties, what will appease his sister and what is best for his children, he chooses the latter. It takes courageous humility, as he faces his children, to follow his heart's reasons. In spite of being torn between two allegiances, he maintains a disciplined grip over his impulsivity. He restrains the impulse, in his emotionally trying state, to slam the door. He pauses in the last minute and shuts it softly. In this pause lies the unique character strength of the man. In the self-humbling humor that follows lies his humanity.

The Encounter-with-the-Lynch-Mob Episode. One of Scout's classmates in school is a boy named Walter Cunningham. Walter's father, also called Walter, is one of her father's clients. Because he is poor and in debt, Atticus tells him not to worry about paying him. Mr. Cunningham pays him intermittently through small amounts of farm goods. The Cunninghams, who live in the surrounding rural area of Old Sarum, are honest, hard-working, uneducated, and poor. They have been hit hard by the economic depression. The Cunninghams, as a large extended family, are also known for their prejudice.

When Atticus's client, Tom Robinson, is transferred to the city jail while awaiting his trial, Atticus, in anticipation of a possible attempt at abduction, decides to guard the entrance to the jail with only a chair, a light, and a newspaper in hand. The children, concerned, locate their father from a hiding distance in the shadows of darkness. A drunken mob from the community of Old Sarum, made up mainly of Cunninghams, descend on the jail with the aim of abducting and lynching Tom Robinson. They ask Atticus to step aside. At that moment, the children, accompanied by Dill, converge on the scene to defend their father. While Atticus is unsuccessfully trying to convince Jem to take his sister and Dill home, one of the members of the mob physically threatens Jem, only to be kicked in a sensitive location by Scout. Her father reminds her not to "kick folks." Scout soon after surveys the group searching for a familiar face and finds one in the person of Mr. Walter Cunningham. She then attempts to engage Mr. Cunningham in a dialogue by inquiring about his entailment (debt situation), with which she was familiar, and about his son Walter, assuring him that he was a good boy at school and that he was her classmate. In search for acknowledgment, she asks if Walter was his boy and if he, the father, remembered her. After a prolonged nonresponsive period, in the midst of surrounding silence and awe-struck, half-opened mouths, Mr. Cunningham "squatted down and took me by both shoulders. 'I'll tell him [my boy] you said hey, little lady,' he said. Then he straightened up and waved a big paw. 'Let's clear out,' he called. 'Let's get going, boys'" (*TKM*, p. 154).

Truly, Scout and Jem are fashioned in their father's image. Scout is her father's daughter. If one meaning of courage is the mastery of fear, then Scout's action is a concrete embodiment of courage. Courageous parents are likely to beget courageous children. Just as Atticus is courageous in attempting to protect his client's life, so is Scout courageous in her protection of her father. In confronting Mr. Cunningham, she awakens in him the more important dimensions of his existence: the caring father and the grateful client. The following morning, in looking back on the dramatic events, Atticus reflects:

> "So it took an eight-year-old child to bring 'em to their senses, didn't it?" said Atticus. "That proves something—that a gang of wild animals *can* be stopped, simply because they're still human . . . you children last night made Walter Cunningham stand in my shoes for a minute. That was enough." . . .
>
> "I don't want either of you bearing a grudge about this thing, no matter what happens." . . .
>
> "Mr. Cunningham's basically a good man," he said, "he just has his blind spots along with the rest of us." (*TKM*, pp. 157–58)

Atticus is imparting two moral lessons to his children. One is about empathetically taking the perspective of the other and viewing him or her as an individual. The other is about the importance of forgiving the frailties of others. It is also a demonstration of how it is more courageous to forgive than to hold a grudge and seek revenge.

The Trial-of-Tom-Robinson Episode. To be courageous is to be courageous about, toward, or on behalf of something or someone we hold dear, precious, or important. Courage does not happen in an abstract vacuum. True courage is about things that matter. Mattering is a prerequisite for genuine courage. Moreover, courage does not mean the absence of apprehension and fear. Daring to the exclusion of apprehensive concern deteriorates into recklessness. Courage may require prolonged living with apprehension or fear. Lastly, courage does not necessarily lead to victory.

All these elements of courage are in evidence in the trial of Tom Robinson. For Atticus Finch, human beings, as individual beings, matter. Deep within, he is propelled by a basic love for humanity. He says to his daughter, on one occasion, "I do my best to love everybody" (*TKM*, p. 108). He will do what it takes to see and treat others kindly and respectfully, as individuals. He wants to defend what is true, right, and fair. In his eyes, everyone is equal under the law. "Our courts have their faults, as does any human institution, but in this country our courts are the great levelers, and in our courts all men are created equal" (*TKM*, p. 205).

But above all, those who matter and touch his heart most are the vulnerable: the children, the poor, and the blacks. Atticus is courageous at home and he never gives in to the natural human impulse of using children as means and not as ends. He never forgets or takes advantage of their precious vulnerability. It is not accidental that he talks to them as adults and they call him by his first name. He is repeatedly described by his children and others as being the same at home, on the street, and in the courtroom. Nothing riles him more than when a (privileged) white man takes advantage of an underprivileged black man. Here is Atticus elucidating the point to his children:

> "The older you grow the more of it you'll see. The one place where a man ought to get a square deal is in a courtroom, be he any color of the rainbow, but people have a way of carrying their resentments right to the jury box. As you grow older, you'll see white men cheat black men every day of your life, but let me tell you something and don't you forget it—whenever a white man does that to a black man, no matter who he is, or how fine a family he comes from, that white man is trash." . . .
>
> "There's nothing more sickening to me than a low-grade white man who'll take advantage of a Negro's ignorance." (*TKM*, pp. 220–21)

Tom Robinson is the embodiment, par excellence, of the vulnerable other. He is a decent, hard-working, gentle, well-mannered, and compassionate soul who felt sympathy, a deadly sin in the Maycomb of the time, for a white woman's need for assistance. He happens to be a poor, uneducated black man. To accentuate his vulnerability, his one arm is partly severed because of an accident with a farming machine. Calpurnia attests to his goodness and his belonging to a clean-living family. He is accused of raping the woman he assisted with house work. His accusers, Bob Ewell and his daughter Mayella Ewell, are known to be "white trash." However, given the climate of the times, the word of decent black men could not measure up even to the words of "white trash." This case, therefore, speaks to the core of Atticus's inner soul.

Atticus Finch knows from the very start what his chances are, close to nil, and what the consequences are, the backlash of a bigoted community. In spite of the odds against him, he aims to give Tom Robinson the best defense of which he is capable. Atticus's description of Mrs. Dubose's courage is at the same time a depiction of his own courage: "It's when you know you're licked before you begin but you begin anyway and you see it through no matter what. You rarely win, but sometimes you do" (*TKM*, p. 112). Although he loses the case and Tom Robinson is convicted of rape, Atticus Finch stands tall in his own eyes, in the eyes of a few good citizens of Maycomb and in the eyes of the black community. Upon the conclusion of the court proceedings, all the blacks, seated in the balcony along with Scout and Jem, stand up when Atticus passes underneath them to leave the courtroom. In the light of this moving moment, the Reverend Sykes says to the seated Scout, "Miss Jean Louise, stand up. Your father's passin'" (*TKM*, p. 211).

Throughout the ordeal surrounding the case Atticus suffers silently. Here is another meaning to courage: To endure the tension of sacrificial suffering undergone as an offering for the sake of a higher cause. Nevertheless, his son Jem, his sister Alexandra, and the good neighbor Miss Maudi sense the toll this case is taking on him. In a conversation with Miss Maudi Atkinson, Aunt Alexandra says,

> "I can't say I approve of everything he does, Maudi, but he's my brother, and I just want to know when this will ever end." Her voice rose: "It tears him to pieces. I've seen him when—what else do they want from him, Maudi, what else?" . . .
> "Have you ever thought of it this way Alexandra? Whether Maycomb knows it or not, we're paying the highest tribute we can pay a man. We trust him to do right. It's that simple." . . .
> "Who" . . .
> "The handful of people in this town who say that fair play is not marked White Only; the handful of people who say a fair trial is for everybody, not just us; the handful of people with enough humility to think, when they look at a Negro, there but for the Lord's kindness am I." (*TKM*, p. 236)

And in a conversation with the children, Miss Maudi tells them, "I simply want to tell you that there are some men in this world who were born to do our unpleasant jobs for us. Your father's one of them" (*TKM*, p. 215).

Before, during, and after the trial, Atticus never allows the tension to spill over into his relationship with his children. Throughout, he remains a consistently concerned and caring parent. He is always there to offer them comfort and soothing solace. He is always there to answer their questions and offer explanations. He does not attempt to overprotectively shield them from the unpleasant and stressful happening around them. He tell Alexandra, "[T]his is their home, sister. . . . We've made it this way for them, they might as well learn to cope with it" (*TKM*, p. 212). He does not prevent them, to the chagrin of his sister, from attending, for the most part, the whole trial proceedings, in which they become intensely involved.

After the trial, Bob Ewell stops Atticus at the post office corner, spits in his face, calls him names, and tells him he'd "get him if it took the rest of his life" (*TKM*, p. 217). When Ewell inquires, "Too proud to fight, you nigger-loving bastard?" Atticus answers, "No, too old," puts his hands in his pockets and strolls on (*TKM*, p. 217). When Atticus is later queried about it, all he says is, "I wish Bob Ewell wouldn't chew tobacco" (*TKM*, p. 217). Hearing about this event, the children learn that there is a higher form of courage in the refusal to fight than in taking on Bob Ewell's lowly challenge.

The Children's-Rescue-by-Boo-Radley-from-Bob-Ewell's-Attack Episode. Soon after the conviction, Tom Robinson is shot by prison guards while attempting to escape, having lost all hope of justice prevailing and despite Atticus's promise of appealing the case. Gradually, things begin to settle down, as Atticus predicted. "[I]n spite of Atticus's shortcomings as a parent [and citizen-lawyer], people were content to reelect him to the state legislature that year, as usual, without opposition" (*TKM*, p. 243). Moreover, although Alexandra remained uneasy about Bob Ewell's threats and a few shadowy actions with which he was either directly or indirectly linked, Atticus felt that Ewell has basically gotten his venom toward him out of Ewell's system.

One night after returning from a Halloween pageant held at the school, and as they were approaching the Radley house, Scout and Jem are attacked by the knife-wielding and drunken Bob Ewell. Hearing the commotion, Boo Radley comes to the rescue and in the process kills Bob Ewell. As a result of the attack, Jem's arm is broken and he is knocked unconscious. Thereafter, Boo Radley carries Jem to the Finch home. Discovering what has happened, Alexandra contacts the doctor and Atticus calls the sheriff. Both are understandably shaken.

The doctor takes care of the broken arm and administers a sedative to enable Jem to rest for the night. The sheriff, Mr. Tate, surveys the scene of the crime and returns to the Finch household. He asks Scout to relate what happened. He then gives his evaluation of the situation. Guided by his wish to protect the integrity of the reclusive Boo Radley, he creates the storyline that Bob Ewell fell on his own knife and killed himself during the attack. Atticus initially and for a while, does not read Mr. Tate's intention accurately. He interprets Tate's story line as a maneuver to protect Jem. But his response to his own misguided interpretation reveals something about Atticus the man and the father:

"Thank you [Mr. Tate] from the bottom of my heart, but I don't want my boy starting out with something like this over his head. Best way to clear the air is to have it all out in the open . . . I don't want him growing up with a whisper about him, I don't want anybody saying, 'Jem Finch . . . his daddy paid a mint to get him out of that.'"

. . .

"If this thing's hushed up it'll be a simple denial to Jem of the way I've tried to raise him. Sometimes I think I'm a total failure as a parent, but I'm all they've got. Before Jem looks at anyone else he looks at me, and I've tried to live so I can look squarely back at him . . . if I connived at something like this, frankly I couldn't meet his eye, and the day I can't do that I'll know I've lost him. I don't want to lose him and Scout, because they're all I've got."

. . .

"[I]f they don't trust me they won't trust anybody. Jem and Scout know what happened. If they hear of me saying downtown something different happened—Heck, I won't have them any more. I can't live one way in town and another way in my home." (*TKM,* pp. 273–74)

Atticus knows that his children look up to him as their model and he wants to remain a good example for them. He also knows that if he leads a life of duplicity, he will lose their trust and ultimately he will lose them.

Atticus agonizingly agrees with Mr. Tate that it is wrong to expose the reclusive Boo Radley to the public. As Mr. Tate puts it, it is like "taking the one man who's done you and this town a great service an' draggin' him with his shy ways into the limelight—to me that's a sin" (*TKM,* p. 276). After Mr. Tate leaves, Atticus contemplates what has transpired for a long while. He then turns to his daughter and says,

"Scout, Mr. Ewell fell on his knife. Can you possibly understand?" Atticus looked like he needed cheering up. I ran to him and hugged him and kissed him with all my might. "Yes sir, I understand," I reassured him. "Mr. Tate was right."

Atticus disengaged himself and looked at me. "What do you mean?"

"Well, it's sort of like shootin' a mockingbird, wouldn't it?"

Atticus put his face in my hair and rubbed it. When he got up and walked across the porch into the shadows, his youthful step had returned. Before he went inside the house, he stopped in front of Boo Radley. "Thank you for my children, Arthur," he said. (*TKM,* p. 276)

In her response to her father, Scout remembers what Atticus had once said soon after she and Jem got children's rifles one Christmas. Atticus cautions them that they can shoot all the blue jays they want, but to never shoot mockingbirds, for that would be a sin. They later learn that the reason is that in their father's eyes mockingbirds bring nothing but joy to people. Similarly, Scout senses the analogy in this context: It is a sin to cause harm to Boo Radley who has not only brought joy but also saved the children's lives. Scout accompanies Boo to his house. She is never to see him again. Upon her return home, she finds her father seated by Jem's bed reading a book. After reading to her a while, she falls asleep. He takes her to her room and puts her to bed. "He turned out the light and went into Jem's room. He would be there all night, and he would be there when Jem waked up in the morning" (*TKM*, p. 281).

Notes

Introduction

1. The phrase "good and loving parents" in this text will have a more comprehensive meaning than, yet can subsume, what in the parenting and human development literature has been described as "authoritative parents" (Baumrind, 1971) or "authoritative-reciprocal parents" (Maccoby and Martin, 1983), "secure-autonomous parents" (Main, 1991, 1996; Cassidy and Shaver, 1999; Karen, 1998) or "securely attached parents" (Grusec et al., 1994; Phelps et al., 1998; Brooks, 2001), and "nurturing parents" (Dacey and Travers, 2002).

Authoritative parents create a context of high nurturance and realistic maturity demands for their children. They are affectionate, fair, firm, and flexible. Their child-rearing style is democratic. They are accepting and warm. Their warmth is coupled with moderate and rational control. While they provide guidance, they communicate clear standards and expect their children to meet them. They monitor their children's behavior without becoming overly involved and intrusive. They allow their children a leeway for making decisions and meeting challenges and obligations. They encourage self-reliance and are sensitive to their children's needs, wishes, competencies, and potentials. They adapt to their children to create a good fit between their parenting practices and routines and their children's unique characteristics. Their disciplinary strategies and practices are nonpunitive in orientation. Their demands are tailored to the children's ability to regulate their own conduct. They serve as sensitive teachers and models to their children. Their pattern of child rearing is labeled "reciprocal" in the sense that their "children are required to be responsible to parental demands, and parents accept a reciprocal responsibility to be as responsive as possible to their children's demands and points of view" (Maccoby and Martin, 1983, p. 46). In essence, the parenting style of authoritative parents is typified by love, limits, guidance, and goodness of fit.

Securely attached parents are consistently responsive to their children's needs. They are attentive and attuned to their children's signals and feeling states. They themselves are emotionally accessible to their children. They are not threatened by their children's negative emotional reactivity. They are warm, accepting, and cooperative. They are emotionally sensitive and supportive of their children. They set clear, consistent, and reasonable standards and limits. Their parenting style is fair and flexible. They are not inclined to misperceive situations and make misat-

133

tributions. As such, they tend to remain sympathetically objective toward their children. As "secure-autonomous" adults, they are able to narrate their life stories in a consistent and convincing fashion. In other words, they are able to give a coherent account of their childhood. They display an open way of reflecting on their early attachments. They have an easy access to a wide range of memories, including positive and negative feelings. They are self-reflective and empathic toward themselves and others. In being open to the point of view of others, they are proficient perspective takers. They have attained balanced objectivity in the way they view their childhood events, positive or negative. If they have experienced harsh or traumatic childhoods or if they have been insecurely attached to their parents, they are able to transcend and accept these early experiences and have "earned" security or secure attachments, which they now value. They have gained distance and are able to place things in perspective. They presently view their parents with understanding and forgiveness. In their relationship to their own parents, they are neither enmeshed, because of the desire to please and seek approval, nor are they cut off, because of cumulative blame, hurt, rage, and resentment. They have worked through these emotions and moved on with their lives.

Nurturing parents are deeply devoted to their children. They are passionately interested in their conduct and welfare. Although they rarely make rules to control their children's behavior, they transmit a clearly defined set of values with the expectation that these values will guide their children's decision making. At the same time, they allow and encourage their children to make decisions and take actions on their own. They rarely punish even when they disapprove of their children's actions. Instead of punishment, they express disappointment. They communicate their point of view through modeling and family discussions. "These parents provide their children with ample opportunities to practice decision-making skills, self-control, and, most vital of all, creative thinking. They serve as caring coaches as their children learn how to live" (Dacey and Travers, 2002, p. 313).

2. When the various contemporary strategies for optimal parenting are compared, certain similarities emerge. According to Hammer and Turner (1996), the "most obvious similarity is the emphasis on a democratic relationship between parents and children, with the child's needs and feelings respected as being valid and as being highly correlated with behavior" (p. 144). Moreover, parental acceptance, nurturance, and warmth are emphasized. Communication is perceived as essential for maintaining and enhancing parent-child relations. Aversive disciplinary techniques (ridiculing, shaming, shouting, threatening, or using physical punishment) are not advocated. Finally, the goal that is implicit in all strategies is raising a responsible child. Parents can help children become more responsible through "providing choices, promoting decision making, being consistent in demands, and emphasizing the needs of parents as well as children. Further, model-

ing of responsible behavior is advocated as a way to foster responsibility in children" (Hammer and Turner, 1996, p. 145).

Although these attributes of optimal parenting are congruent with the dimensions of good and loving parenting described in this book, they are not grounded in a rigorous theory of human existence. Yet, they may be viewed as being incipiently rooted in an intuitive understanding of what it means to be good human beings.

3. The term *existential,* has multiple meanings. The noun version, "existence," is derived from the Latin "ex" and "sistere," which means to emerge. As existential beings, therefore, we are always emerging or becoming our true essential selves. An existential psychological theory, then, views human beings as unique individuals who are always, under optimal conditions, becoming their authentic selves. An existential psychological approach aims at understanding how individuals confront and come to terms with the dualities or polarities of human existence: life vs. death; agency vs. communion; good vs. evil; holding on vs. letting go; control vs. surrender; and many more (see Deurzen-Smith, 1988, 1997; Deurzen, 1998). Existential psychology tries to comprehend the strategies persons use to cope with anxiety over inevitable choice making, ontological insecurity, and death. It aims to understand how we deal with our guilt over not being the persons we could have become and over not understanding and consequently harming others and ultimately ourselves. It tries to clarify how we make meaning in the face of meaninglessness; how we assume, or fail in the assumption of, responsibility; and how we deal with our aloneness, loneliness, and isolation.

Because of the nature of our human existence, we are inevitably suspended between polarities. Polarities, says Daniel Levinson (1978), "exist during the entire life cycle" (p. 198). This state of suspension generates a dialectic: a tension-filled tendency to move between opposite forces. These opposing forces "define each other or lend meaning to each other (Without hate there can be no love)" (Wrightsman, 1994, p. 150). "Personality development reflects striving toward fulfillment or achievement of each of these forces and separate from the other. These characteristics can be thought of as needs to be met" (Wrightsman, 1994, pp. 150–51). As humans, we all struggle, for example, to meet our needs for dependence and independence. We will experience inevitable tensions in our quest to meet these opposing needs. Levinson (1978) believes that they "can never be resolved or transcended" (p. 198). But "achieving a [relative] synthesis between oppositional forces [or needs], lead[s] . . . to a higher level of [personality] integration" (Wrightsman, 1994, p. 159). Because of these oppositional forces, tension or conflict is of the essence of human existence. Conflicts and tensions motivate us to continue to change and grow. There are times when we have to endure contradictions and irresolvable conflicts.

In this text, the existential approach is applied toward understanding the essential dimensions of good and loving parenting. An existential theory of parenting, which is a variation on an existential theory of becoming human, seeks to answer ultimate questions such as What can parents do to make children feel welcome in the world, to feel like they belong in this world, to feel at home in the world? What kind of persons ought parents aspire to be in order to affirm the essential worth and preciousness of their children, in order to radiate a sense of awe, wonder, and joy in the presence of their children, in order to create a home atmosphere that is filled with laughter, love, and learning? What kind of unfolding story or fate are they living out in their everyday transactions with their children? Are they accepting of their unfolding fate, while at the same time attempting to stretch its boundaries? How do they come to terms with the guilt and shame they experience as a consequence of not being the persons they ought to become in their interactions with their children? What do parents teach their children, directly through instruction or indirectly through modeling, about forgiveness, tolerance, suffering, wickedness, and evil? How do parents go about cultivating and nourishing the goodness of character in their children? How do parents embody and transmit the virtues of courage, good judgment, humility, nobility, piety, and wisdom to their children? How do parents confront and come to terms with their limitations, vulnerabilities, and weaknesses as their children observe them? How do parents take up that which is trivial, unimportant, or blindly conventional? How much self-deception or deception of others do parents engage in as they interact with and are observed by their children? How authentic and genuine are they in their relations to their children? How do parents confront the dualities of their own and those of their children's existence (dualities such as dependence versus independence, separateness versus connectedness)? How do parents make use of their competencies, strengths, and talents?

An existential theory of parenting will attempt to provide answers to these types of questions. The aim of this book is to make use of insights from developmental psychology, self psychology, moral philosophy, and existential philosophy in an effort to answer the ultimate question that subsumes all other questions: What does it mean to become good and loving parents/persons? It is also hoped that when this meaning is taken up by the reader, it will lead to a movement, small as it may be, toward perfect (excellent or good) parenting.

4. What the British pediatrician and psychoanalyst D. W. Winnicott (1965) has coined as the *good-enough mother* is to be subsumed under what is described in this text as the *good/loving parent*. Winnicott describes "good-enough mothers" as parents who provide sufficiently for what their children need, at different developmental periods, to give them a good start in life. They are able to adapt and change accordingly to the changing needs of their children. Gradually, their children become less dependent on them. Good-enough mothers have an abundance of empathic caregiving ability. When they first become mothers, they are preoccupied with the needs of their babies. Winnicott calls this "primary maternal preoccupation." They experience their infants as parts of themselves.

Gradually, mothers resume their own independence, as their children become less demanding of them. Good-enough mothers initially nurture their infants' sense of omnipotence by responding to their vocalizations, gestures, and demands. The infants come to sense that their environment is magically under their control. As they grow and experience manageable disillusionment, they let go of their omnipotence and thus become more realistic in their demands. Gradually they move from an unconscious state of symbiosis to conscious differentiation and individuation.

    5. Attachment theory was developed by John Bowlby and Mary Ainsworth. Attachment theorists distinguish between "attachment" and "attachment behaviors." *Attachment* refers to an enduring affectional or emotional tie between infants and their caregivers. "Indeed, to Bowlby, attachment was much closer to the idea of love, if not identical with it" (Karen, 1998, p. 90). For Bowlby, to be attached, to love and be loved is biologically based. It is built into the nature of human infants. It is grounded in human evolutionary heritage. The propensity toward attachment has contributed to the survival of the human species. Children need to be lovingly attached to their primary caregivers in order to feel safe, secure, and protected. "[T]o be attached, even anxiously attached, is to be in love" (Karen, 1998, p. 230). Attachment theorists make a distinction between "secure" and "insecure" (anxious) attachment. The essence of attachment theory lies on the premise that when primary caregivers are fairly consistently responsive to children's signals and needs and are respectful of their need for independent exploration of the environment, children will become securely attached and will consequently develop an internal (mental) model of the self as competent, valued, and self-reliant and of essential others as lovingly available, trustworthy, and reliable. This internal "working" model is dynamic and can change over time. However, the early years are critical for its formation. It continually guides children's relational expectations. At times it has been referred to by attachment theorists and researchers as "an internal template of love." Bowlby (1973) writes, "in the working model of the world that anybody builds, a key feature is his notion of who his attachment figures are, where they may be found, and how they may be expected to respond" (p. 203).

    Attachment behaviors are rooted in our biological nature and are essential for security and survival. The aim of attachment behaviors, whether displayed by infants (e.g., crying, cooing, or smiling) or adults (holding hands or hugging), is to secure and maintain proximity to an essential other. "[P]roximity begets feelings of love, security, and joy" (Karen, 1998, pp. 90–91).

    Attachment theory holds, then, that children who consistently and reliably receive love, are made to feel that they are lovable and have fundamental worth, and whose needs are for the most part significantly met become *securely attached.* Securely attached children have faith in the parents' love. They trust their own ability to get tender loving care when needed. They feel free to explore the environment. They have confidence in their competence. They "love their parents powerfully and need to have that love returned and sustained" (Karen, 1998, p. 397).

Our need to love and be loved remains with us throughout the life cycle. "[H]uman beings of all ages are happiest and able to deploy their talents to best advantage," writes Bowlby (1979), "when they are confident that, standing behind them there are one or more trusted persons who will come to their aid should difficulties arise" (p. 103). "All of us," continues Bowlby (1988), "from the cradle to the grave, are happiest when life is organized as a series of excursions long or short, from a secure base provided by our attachment figure(s)" (p. 62).

6. The *nature-versus-nurture issue* is an old controversy among developmental theorists. Exemplifying such rivalries in the 1930s and the 1940s are psychologists Arnold Gesell (1880–1961) and John B. Watson (1878–1958). Gesell (1933) views development as a genetically determined process that unfolds automatically, just like a flower. He argues that human development is mostly a matter of biological maturation. Biological maturation means that the process of development is directed from within by the action of the genes. Individual differences in growth rates are mostly due to internal genetic influences. The social environment can facilitate optimal development by synchronizing with these inner maturational principles. Development, therefore, follows an inner biological plan. The environment merely supports this inner unfolding of biologically based behavioral patterns. Louise Bates Ames (1971), one of Gesell's followers, advises parents to "[g]ive up the notion that how your child turns out is all up to you and there isn't a minute to waste" (p. 108).

For John B. Waston (1928), infants and children do not have inborn tendencies. There are no blueprints for behavioral patterns that unfold according to an inner biological plan of maturation. Behavioral patterns are nothing more than stimulus-response connections (habits) that are ultimately under environmental control. According to Watson, the way children turn out is largely up to parents in particular and the social environment in general. Parents are mostly responsible for what their children will become. The kind of persons children become is a by-product of the habits they cultivate. Watson urged parents to instill good habits in their children.

Watson wanted to transform child rearing into a scientific endeavor. He suggested to parents to remain "objective" in their approach to their children. He further recommended to them to abstain from caressing, hugging, or kissing their babies. He felt that such indulgent associations discouraged children from becoming independent and self-sufficient and from exploring the environment on their own. He, therefore, cautioned against building strong emotional bonds between parents and children.

Watson's recommendations regarding child rearing went beyond what his behavioristic research and principles could support. They were colored by his own idiosyncratic, personal, and cultural biases (see Hannush, 1983). Still, his child-rearing strategies were popular in the 1930s and the 1940s. His advice had a simple practical and "scientific" ring to it: To become a good parent, all you have to do is to build good habits in your children.

Watson, along with his second wife, Rosalie Rayner, tried to practice what he preached on their two sons, William and James. Here is James B. Watson reflecting on his father's behavioristic parenting practices:

> I have some unhappy thoughts about my upbringing . . . about the effect of behavioristic principles on my being raised into an adult. It is difficult not to let these thoughts affect my feelings about my father. In many ways I adored him as an individual and as a character. He had a nice sense of humor. He was bright; he was charming; he was masculine, witty, reflective. But he was also conversely unresponsive, . . . unable to express and cope with any feelings of emotion of his own, and determined unwittingly to deprive, I think, my brother and me of any kind of emotional foundation. . . . We were never kissed or held as children; we were never shown any kind of emotional closeness. (Hannush, 1987, pp. 137–38)

William, the older brother, became a psychiatrist, underwent many years of psychoanalytic therapy for manic-depression, and subsequently committed suicide. James, after completing a college degree in industrial psychology and after undergoing years of analytic therapy for depression, became a successful executive with Hunt-Wesson Foods. As children, William and James were also inevitably affected by the untimely death of their mother at the age of 35.

Watson's strict, Spartan, and so-called scientific approach to and advice on parenting was too extreme and historically regressive to withstand the test of time. Under the influence of Spock, the Americanized Freud, and Bowlby, parents moved toward becoming more relaxed, affectionate, and empathically attuned with their children. "Nevertheless, Watson's more general goal—that of placing child training on the firm foundation of scientific learning principles—remains a vital part of child care in the United States" (Crain, 2000, p. 176). Moreover, that Watson heightened the attention of countless parents to the influence of their parenting practices on their children cannot be denied. Similarly, Spock, who in turn was influenced by Gesell, helped millions in becoming better parents, in small part, by telling them "to trust themselves" and "that they know more than they think and that they should follow their impulses to respond to their babies' needs" (Crain, 2000, p. 275).

7. My own maternal grandmother, who was neither a great saint nor a spiritual leader, who lived with my family during my formative years, and who had been orphaned as a child as a consequence of the genocide of the Armenians and the Assyrians in Turkey, lived the life of an ordinary saint amongst us. She

demonstrated her transcendence of her tragic past by the way she lived her life. A woman of strong and deep faith, she was the embodiment of the virtues of gentleness, humility, self-sacrifice, and selfless love.

In his autobiographical work, *Black Boy,* Richard Wright (1966) demonstrates how he was able to rise above his difficult and traumatic childhood. Even though he was subjected to constant devaluation of his personhood and threats to his physical safety during his formative years, he found refuge in the world of books which alerted him to the possibility of living without anger, fear, and hunger. Through reading and later writing, he was able to assert himself and give voice to a differently imagined world. Throughout, he tried not to compromise his sense of right and wrong. See Hannush (1985) for an extensive analysis of Wright's autobiography.

Chapter One. Growth in Parenting

1. The work of Erik Erikson (1963, 1964, 1968, 1980, 1982) is interpreted and revisioned in the light of an existential theory of parenting. For other theoretical extensions of the work of Erikson, the works of Browning (1975), McAdams (2001), and Newman and Newman (1999) are recommended to the reader.

2. The compatibility of Eriksonian theory and evolutionary theory can be demonstrated directly and indirectly. According to Erikson, human beings experience a biologically based urge to pro(create) and to take care of that which they pro(create). Parenting is one way through which human beings satisfy these needs, and thus extend their genetic heritage into the future.

Indirectly, Erikson's theory is compatible with attachment theory (see the discussion on attachment theory in the introduction), which itself is grounded in evolutionary theory. Erikson's description of "basic trust" is very congruent with Bowlby's description of "secure attachment." According to Erikson, parents who, for the most part, respond consistently to their infants' needs will foster a sense of basic trust in other people. This will enable children to form close affectional ties with other people later in life. Both Bowlby and Erikson believe that the availability, responsiveness, and affection of parents promote feelings of warmth, security, and trust in their infants. The basic trust they gain from this secure attachment sets the stage for healthy psychosocial development throughout life. John Bowlby (1973, 1979, 1982, 1988) goes beyond Erikson by positing an "internal working model." Bowlby believes that as infants and children continue to interact with their parents, they develop a cognitive representation of themselves and other people. They use these internal working models to interpret their interpersonal world and to form expectations about the nature of human relationships. Securely attached and trusting children develop positive working models.

Galatzer-Levy and Cohler (1993) suggest that we may "not need the complex idea that the child must make a mental model of the good care she received"

(p. 84) to explain secure attachment and its cognitive, behavioral, and affective consequences. An alternative explanation is that "more securely attached children tend to be better organized, which may lead to more coherent performances in all areas" (p. 84). These two alternative models are not necessarily mutually exclusive, although one seems more parsimonious than the other.

3. These are reflective of Abraham Maslow's (1970) hierarchy of needs.

4. There is a "selfish" as well as selfless or self-sacrificing component in generative care. "One of the most fascinating aspects of generativity is its conflictual [paradoxical] essence—it celebrates the infinite expansion of the self and the surrender of the self at the same time" (McAdams, 2001, p. 580). "For example," continues McAdams,

> The truly generative father is both a self-aggrandizing creator and a self-sacrificing giver. Biologically and socially, he creates a child in his own image, working hard and long to promote the development of the child and to nurture all that is good and desirable in the child. But he must eventually grant the child his or her own autonomy, letting go when the time is right, letting the child develop his or her own identity, make his or her own decisions and commitments, and ultimately create those offerings of generativity that will distinguish that child as someone who was "given birth to" in order to "give birth to." (p. 581)

5. What Erikson calls "pseudospeciation," Goodall (1999) terms as "cultural speciation." Regardless, the aim is the same: to constrict and place boundaries around one's circle of care and to view others who are outside the circle as different, inferior, and threatening.

6. Erikson equated generativity with psychological health and psychosocial maturity. Research reported by McAdams (2001) and longitudinal studies conducted by Vaillant (1977) and Snary (1993) have supported Erikson's equation of generativity with optimal psychosocial adaptation and psychological wellness.

7. Erikson emphasizes that adults do not have to be parents in order to be generative. Generative adults, however, display a different parenting style than less generative adults. When Peterson and Klohnen (1995) compared generative mothers to less generative mothers, they found that generative mothers were significantly more invested and committed in their parenting life project and showed an "expanded radius of care." Moreover, their parenting style was *authoritative* in approach (see note 1 in the introduction). Research by Baumrind and others has shown that children of authoritative parents have greater self-esteem, achieve higher levels of moral development, and are more socially competent than children of non-authoritative parents—parents who are either permissive/negligent or authoritarian.

Chapter Two. Parenting as Care

1. The work of Heinz Kohut (1971, 1977, 1978, 1984) is interpreted and revisioned in the light of an existential theory of parenting. For secondary sources on Kohut's self psychology, the works of Berzoff, Flanagan, and Hertz (1996), St. Clair (1996), and Wolf (1988) are recommended to the reader.

2. Empathy, or feeling with, and, later, understanding the emotional configuration of another, has been linked to the quality of parenting. Whereas empathic, secure/autonomous, and authoritative parents beget empathic children, nonempathic, authoritarian, negligent, and abusive parents beget non-empathic children (Eisenberg and McNally, 1993; Klimes-Dougan and Kistner, 1990; Koestner, Franz, and Weinberger, 1990; Weinfield, Sroufe, Egeland, and Carlson, 1999).

3. Heinz Kohut's concept of "mirroring" is remarkably close to Carl Rogers's (1961, 1980) concept of "unconditional positive regard." From a Rogerian viewpoint, children need to be liked, prized, and unconditionally accepted. They thrive when enveloped by their parents' nonpossessive warmth. In the relative absence of conditions of worth, they are allowed to be themselves. They feel accepted without reservations or restrictions. Their basic value or worth is not experienced as being contingent on specific performances.

Interestingly, both Kohut and Rogers emphasize the importance of empathy or empathic listening. Kohut calls it "vicarious introspection." To Rogers (1980) empathy "means temporarily living the other's life, moving about in it delicately without making judgments" (p. 142). Kohut and Rogers both believe that empathic listening fosters personal growth and wholeness. Applied to the parenting context, this means that when children are empathically listened to by their parents, they come to feel more solid and integrated.

Lastly, Rogers's concept of "congruence" has important relevance for what it means to become good parents. To be congruent, for Rogers, means to be genuine, real, integrated, and whole; it is to be what one truly is. Congruent parents do not act as though they were something they are not. They do not put on facades. They are not duplicitous. What they say matches how they feel. They are in touch with what is going on inside them. And just as there are degrees of unconditional positive regard and empathy, so too there are degrees of congruence. Parents who provide their children with high degrees of unconditional positive regard, empathic listening, and congruence create optimal conditions for their children to become themselves. For a comparative analysis of the convergence between the therapeutic approaches of Rogers and Kohut, see Kahn (1997).

4. From a Kohutian standpoint, children are likely to experience fragmentation when parents (a) fail to be empathically attuned to their physical, emotional, and psychosocial needs; (b) fail to mirror their grandiose or expansive tendencies and help them transform these natural proclivities into realistic and

realizable ambitions; (c) fail to become idealizable figures for their children with whom they can identify and thus feel similarly connected to. Different degrees of cumulative parental failures cause children to acquire different levels of maturity. Kohut views *narcissism* in terms of these different levels of maturity. Degrees of fragmentation are commensurate with levels of immaturity. Children with an unhealthy sense of narcissism are likely to experience helplessness, emptiness, shame, rage, and lowered self-esteem.

5. The moral emotions of shame and guilt have aptly been labeled by Michael Lewis (1993) as the self-conscious emotions. Along with the feeling of pride, they are experienced with the gradual emergence of self-awareness. They require a reflexive attunement to the evaluations of the developing self by others and, later, a capacity for self-evaluation. They can be viewed as the emotional barometers of the level of maturity of the emerging self. Pride is experienced as a consequence of the enhancement of the self. Shame and guilt are experienced as a result of an injury or harm done to self and others or as a result of violating one's own or others' ideals for the self, or finally, as a result of violating rules or standards of conduct. For a further discussion of the moral or self-conscious emotions, see Damon (1988) and Harter (1999).

Although "the word 'shame' is rarely if ever used" in the literature on attachment theory and research, "shameful feelings about the self are an important component of relational insecurity" (Karen, 1998, p. 238). Attachment theory holds that when children do not get love reliably and consistently, they are made to feel that they are not worthy of love or respect. The child "is in effect, ashamed of what he [or she] is" (Karen, 1998, P. 239). When children's needs are not met, when their feelings are not attuned to, they become insecurely attached. "The very fact of not being attuned to, so central [a] feature of anxious attachment, is in itself a shame-inducing experience" (Karen, 1998, p. 239). Children who are degraded, devalued, neglected, rejected, and are made to feel worthless come to feel unwanted, undesirable, unlovable, and ugly. "This sense of deformity, degradation, or worthlessness is a central feature of shame" (Karen, 1998, p. 239). The appropriate label for this kind of primordial feeling about the self is *existential shame*. Children with this self-feeling are ashamed of existing.

6. Martin Hoffman (1981) makes the assertion that there is a biological foundation for the gradual emergence of altruistic brehavior. According to Hoffman, even infants are able to display empathy—able to recognize and experience the emotions of others. When infants hear a real infant crying, they soon after begin to cry themselves and show physical signs of agitation and distress. For Hoffman, the capacity for empathy, which is present at birth, is a precursor of altruism.

7. See for example, Hermans and Kempen (1993) and McAdams (1993).

8. The concept of self-efficacy bridges nicely the constructs of self-concept and self-esteem. No psychologist has researched this concept more rigorously than

Albert Bandura (1997). According to Bandura, children learn by selectively imitating models (essential others) who are perceived as affectionate, nurturing,
rewarding, powerful, and similar to themselves. Moreover, by observing these
essential others engage in self-praise and self-blame and through the feedback they
receive about the worth of their own actions, children acquire standards of conduct and a sense of *self-efficacy*. Self-efficacious children believe that their own
abilities and characteristics will be instrumental in their success. They believe that
they have the behavioral skills needed for success in a given situation. They hold
the conviction that they have what it takes to reach their goals. They have
confidence in their behavioral competence. Children with a high sense of self-
efficacy have a history of prior successes and anticipate future successes. They are
able to turn off negative thoughts associated with potential failure, are not turned
off by risky situations in which they might fail or perform lower than expected ,
and are not overwhelmingly aroused by challenging tasks.

Interestingly, self-efficacy has been linked to secure attachment (Weinfield,
Sroufe, Egeland, and Carlson, 1999). In other words, securely attached children
are likely to have a high sense of self-efficacy.

Chapter Three. The Moral Dimension of Parenting

1. The work of Iris Murdoch (1971, 1993, 1998) is interpreted and revisioned in the light of an existential theory of parenting. For secondary sources on
Murdoch's moral philosophy, the works of O'Connor (1996) and Ramanathan
(1990) are recommended to the reader.

Chapter Four. Parenting as an Existential Life Project

1. The work of Michael Gelven (1990, 1991, 1996, 1997, 1998, 2000) is
interpreted and revisioned in the light of an existential theory of parenting.
2. Gelven makes a distinction between negative and positive innocence.
"Negative innocence is the inability to be held responsible for wrongdoing; positive innocence is the preciousness that is found in the realization that who we are
matters independently of behavior" (Gelven, 1998, p. 72).

Chapter Five. Empowerment in Parenting

1. The work of Rollo May (1953, 1969, 1972, 1975, 1981, 1983, 1985) is
interpreted and revisioned in the light of an existential theory of parenting. This
chapter is based in part on an article by the author (Hannush, 1999a) on Rollo
May's theory of human development. The author (Hannush 1999b) has also
conducted an interview with Rollo May.

2. In the novel *Great Expectations* by Charles Dickens (2001), the two protagonists, Estella and Pip, experience reversals of fortune, as their lives unfold from childhood into adulthood. The poor Pip is recruited to become the playmate for the spoiled but rich Estella. Estella's adoptive mother, Miss Havisham, for whom life has lost its meaning subsequent to the betrayal of her would-be husband on her wedding day, raises her secretively adopted but exceptionally beautiful daughter to break the hearts of boys and men and thus gain her due revenge. Being a dutiful daughter, Estella is cruel to and manipulative of the lovelorn Pip. As she becomes of age, she breaks Pip's heart and marries an affluent man with social standing, in spite of Pip's warning that the man had a bad character. When Pip experiences a second reversal of fortune, he travels overseas to earn a decent living. Having never forgotten his first love, and having never married, he hears that the man she married turned out to be abusive, squandered the family fortunes, and subsequently died in a horsing accident. Pip returns home for a visit.

Dickens has written two endings for this novel. In the published version, the two protagonists unite and never part. In the original version, they remain apart, in spite of a brief encounter in the streets of London.

In the published version, Pip decides, in rememberance of Estella, to visit the home of the late Miss Havisham, which now lies in ruins. There, by coincidence, he stumbles upon Estella, who also has come to see her childhood home before it is completely torn down. Here is a part of the concluding dialogue:

> "Suffering has been stronger than all other teaching, and has taught me [Estella] to understand what your heart used to be. I have been *bent and broken, but—I hope—into a better shape.* Be as considerate and good to me as you were, and tell me we are friends."
>
> "We are friends," said I [Pip]. . . ." (Dickens, 2001, p. 433; emphasis added)

Here is the original conclusion, which Dickens decided not to publish based upon the advice of a respected friend:

> I [Pip] was very glad to have had the interview [with Estella]; for, in her face and in her voice, and in her touch, she gave me the assurance, that suffering had been stronger than Miss Havisham's teaching, and had given her a heart to understand what my heart used to be. (Dickens, 2001, p. 438)

Chapter Six. Parenting and the Life of the Spirit

1. Once again the work of Michael Gelven (1990, 1991, 1996, 1997, 1998, 2000) is interpreted and revisioned in the light of an existential theory of parenting.

2. Over Immanuel Kant's grave are inscribed his words: "The starry heavens above me; the moral law within me."

Appendix. The Story of To Kill a Mockingbird *Revisited*

1. For a secondary source on Harper Lee's *To Kill a Mockingbird,* the work of Johnson (1994) is recommended to the reader.

References

Ames, L. B. (1971). Don't push your preschooler. *Family Circle Magazine* 79, 60.

Ainsworth, M., and J. Bowlby. (1991). An ethological approach to personality. *American Psychologist* 46, 333–41.

Bandura, A. (1986). *Social foundations of thought and action: A social cognitive theory.* Englewood Cliffs, N.J.: Prentice Hall.

———. (1997). *Self-efficacy: The exercise of control.* New York: Freeman.

Baumrind, D. (1971). Current patterns of parental authority. *Developmental Psychology Monographs* 4, 1–103.

———. (1993). The average expectable environment is not good enough: A response to Scarr. *Child Development* 64, 1299–1317.

Beck, L. W. (1960). *A commentary on Kant's critique of practical reason.* Chicago: University of Chicago Press.

Berk, L. E. (2001). *Development through the lifespan* (2d ed.). Boston: Allyn and Bacon.

Berzoff, J., L. M. Flanagan, and P. Hertz. (1996). *Inside out and outside in: Psychodynamic clinical theory and practice in contemporary multicultural contexts.* Northvale, N.J.: Jason Aronson.

Bowlby, J. (1973). *Attachment and loss. Vol. 2: Separation.* New York: Basic Books.

———. (1979). *The making and breaking of affectional bonds.* New York: Routledge.

———. (1982). *Attachment and loss. Vol. 1: Attachment* (rev. ed.). New York: Basic Books.

———. (1988). *A secure base.* New York: Basic Books.

Brooks, J. B. (2001). *Parenting* (3d ed.). Mountain View, Calif.: Mayfield.

Browning, D. S. (1975). *Generative man: Psychoanalytic perspectives.* New York, Dell.

Byatt, A. S. (1996). *The Matisse stories.* New York: Random House.

Cassidy, J., and P. R. Shaver (eds.). (1999). *Handbook of attachment: Theory, research, clinical applications.* New York: Guilford.

Crain, W. (2000). *Theories of development: Concepts and applications* (4th ed.). Upper Saddle River, N.J.: Prentice Hall.

Dacey, J. S., and J. F. Travers. (2002). *Human development across the lifespan* (5th ed.). New York: McGraw-Hill.

Damon, W. (1988). *The moral child: Nurturing children's natural moral growth.* New York: Free Press.

deMause, L. (ed.). (1974). *The history of childhood.* New York: Harper and Row.

Deurzen-Smith, E. van (1988). *Existential counseling in practice.* London: Sage.

———. (1997). *Everyday mysteries: Existential dimensions of psychotherapy.* New York: Routledge.

Deurzen, E. van. (1998). *Passion and paradox in psychotherapy: An existential approach to therapy and counseling.* New York: Wiley.

Dickens, C. (2001). *Great expectations.* New York: Modern Library.

Dreikurs, R. (1964). *Children: The challenge.* New York: Hawthorn/Dutton.

Eisenberg, N., and S. McNally. (1993). Socialization and mothers' and adolescents' empathy-related characteristics. *Journal of Research on Adolescence* 3, 171–91.

Eliot, G. (1966). *Silas Marner.* New York: Everyman's Library/Dutton.

Erikson, E. H. (1963). *Childhood and society* (2d ed.). New York: W. W. Norton.

———. (1964). *Insight and responsibility.* New York: W. W. Norton.

———. (1968). *Identity: Youth and crisis.* New York: W. W. Norton

———. (1980). *Identity and the life cycle.* New York: W. W. Norton.

———. (1982). *The life cycle completed.* New York; W. W. Norton.

Faber, A., and E. Mazlish. (1980). *How to talk so kids will listen and listen so kids will talk.* New York: Avon.

Galinsky, E. (1981). *Between generations: The six stages of parenthood.* New York: Times Books.

Galatzer-Levy, R. M., and B. J. Cohler. (1993). *The essential other: A developmental psychology of the self.* New York: Basic Books.

Gelven, M. (1990). *Truth and existence: A philosophical inquiry.* University Park: Pennsylvania State University Press.

———. (1991). *Why me? A philosophical inquiry into fate.* DeKalb: Northern Illinois University Press.

———. (1996). *The quest for the fine: A philosophical inquiry into judgment, worth, and existence.* Lanham, Md: Rowman and Littlefield.

———. (1997). *The risk of being: What it means to be good and bad.* University Park: Pennsylvania State University Press.

———. (1998). *This side of evil.* Milwaukee, Wisc.: Marquette University Press.

———. (2000). *The asking mystery: A philosophical inquiry.* University Park: The Pennsylvania State University Press.

Gesell, A. (1933). Maturation and the patterning of behavior. In C. Murchison (ed.), *A handbook of child psychology.* Worcester, Mass.: Clark University Press.

Goodall, J. (with P. Berman). (1999). *Reason for hope: A spiritual journey.* New York: Warner Books.

Gordon, T. (1975). *Parent effectiveness training.* New York: New American Library.

Grusec. J. E., P. Hastings, and N. Mammone. (1994). Parenting cognitions and relationship schemes. In J. G. Smetena (ed.), *Beliefs about parenting: Origins and developmental implications,* (pp. 5–19). San Francisco: Jossey-Bass.

Hammer, T. J., and P. H. Turner. (1996). *Parenting in contemporary society* (3d ed.). Boston: Allyn and Bacon.

Hannush, M. J. (1983). The mirage of value-neutrality in the behaviorisms of J. B. Watson and B. F. Skinner: The nature of the relationship between personal and professional value areas. *Journal of Phenomenological Psychology* 14, 43–90.

———. (1985). The methodology of phenomenological psychobiography: The case of Richard Wright's *Black Boy* revisited. *Journal of Phenomenological Psychology* 16, 39–86.

———. (1987). John B. Watson remembered: An interview with James B. Watson. *Journal of the History of the Behavioral Sciences* 23, 137–52.

———. (1999a). The development of the self in the light of the existential-humanistic psychology of Rollo May. *Review of Existential Psychology and Psychiatry* 24, 73–103.

———. (1999b). An interview with Rollo May. *Review of Existential Psychology and Psychiatry* 24, 129–41.

Harris, J. R. (1998). *The nurture assumption: Why children turn out the way they do.* New York: Free Press.

Harter, S. (1999). *The construction of the self: A developmental perspective.* New York: Guilford.

Hermans, H. J. M., and H. J. G. Kempen. (1993). *The dialogical self: Meaning and movement.* San Diego: Academic.

Hoffman, M. L. (1981). Is altruism part of human nature? *Journal of Personality and Social Psychology* 40, 121–37.

Johnson, C. D. (1994). *To Kill A Mockingbird: Threatening boundaries,* New York: Twayne.

Kagan, J. (1984). *The nature of the child.* New York: Basic Books.

Kahn, M. (1997). *Between therapist and client: The new relationship* (rev. ed.). New York: W. H. Freeman.

Kant, I. (1956). *Critique of practical reason.* (Lewis White Beck, Trans.). New York: Liberal Arts Press.

Karen, R. (1998). *Becoming attached: First relationships and how they shape our capacity to love.* New York: Oxford University Press.

Klimes-Dougan, B., and J. Kistner. (1990). Physically abused preschoolers' responses to peers' distress. *Developmental Psychology* 26, 599–602.

Koestner, R., C. Franz, and J. Weinberger. (1990). The family origins of empathic concern: A twenty-six-year longitudinal study. *Journal of Personality and Social Psychology* 58, 709–17.

Kohut, H. (1971). *The analysis of the self.* New York: International Universities Press.

———. (1977). *The restoration of the self.* New York: International Universities Press.

———. (1978). *The search for the self.* New York: International Universities Press.

————. (1984). *How does analysis cure?* Chicago: University of Chicago Press.

Langer, S. (1977). *Feeling and form.* Paramus, N.J.: Prentice Hall.

Lee, H. (1960). *To Kill a Mockingbird.* New York: Warner Books.

Levinson, D. J. (1978). *The seasons of a man's life.* New York: Knopf.

Lewis, M. (1993). Self-conscious emotions: Embarrassment, pride, shame, and guilt. In M. Lewis and J. M. Haviland (eds.), *Handbook of emotions.* New York: Plenum.

Lickona, T. (1983). *Raising good children: From birth through the teenage years.* New York: Bantam Books.

Loevinger, J. (1959). Patterns of parenthood as theories of learning. *Journal of Abnormal and Social Psychology* 59, 148–50.

Maccoby, E. E., and J. A. Martin. (1983). Socialization in the context of the family: Parent-child interactions. In P. H. Mussen (ed.), *Handbook of child psychology: Vol. 4* (4th ed., pp. 1–102). New York: Wiley.

Main, M. (1991). Metacognitive knowledge, metacognitive monitoring, and singular (coherent) vs. multiple (incoherent) model of attachment. In C. M. Parkes, J. Stevenson-Hinde, and P. Marris (eds.), *Attachment across the life cycle* (pp. 127–59). London: Tavistock/Routledge.

————. (1996, April). Introduction to the special section on attachment and psychopathology: Overview of the field of attachment. *Journal of Consulting and Clinical Psychology* 64 (2), 237–42.

Martin, C. A., and K. K. Colbert. (1997). *Parenting: A life span perspective.* New York: McGraw-Hill.

Maslow, A. (1970). *Motivation and personality* (2d ed.). New York: Harper and Row.

May, R. (1953). *Man's search for himself.* New York: Dell.

————. (1969). *Love and will.* New York: Dell.

————. (1972). *Power and innocence.* New York: W. W. Norton.

————. (1975). *The courage to create.* New York: W. W. Norton.

————. (1981). *Freedom and destiny.* New York: W. W. Norton.

————. (1983). *The discovery of being.* New York: W. W. Norton.

————. (1985). *My quest for beauty.* Dallas, Tex.: Saybrook.

McAdams, D. P. (1993). *The stories we live by: Personal myths and the making of the self.* New York: William Morrow.

————. (2001). *The person: An integrated introduction to personality psychology* (3d ed.). Fort Worth, Tex.: Harcourt.

Murdoch, I. (1971). *The sovereignty of good.* New York: Schocken Books.

————. (1993). *Metaphysics as a guide to morals.* New York: Allen Lane/Penguin.

————. (1998). *Existentialists and mystics.* New York: Allen Lane/Penquin Press.

Newman, B. M., and P. R. Newman. (1999). *Development through life: A psychosocial approach* (7th ed.). Belomont, Calif.: Wadsworth.

O'Connor, P. J. (1996). *To love the good: The moral philosophy of Iris Murdoch.* New York: Peter Lang.

Peterson, B. E., and E. C. Klohnen. (1995). Realization of generativity in two samples of women at midlife. *Psychology and Aging* 10, 20–29.

Phelps, J. L., J. Belsky, and K. Crnic. (1998). Earned security, daily hassles, and parenting: A comparison of five alternative models. *Development and Psychopathology* 10, 21–38.

Ramanathan, S. (1990). *Iris Murdoch: Figures of good.* New York: St. Martin's.

Reeves, C. (1977). *The psychology of Rollo May.* San Francisco: Jossey-Bass.

Rogers, C. R. (1961). *On becoming a person.* Boston: Houghton Mifflin.

———. (1980). *A way of being.* Boston: Houghton Mifflin.

Scarr, S. (1992). Developmental theories for 1990s: Development and individual differences. *Child Development* 63, 1–19.

Snary, J. (1993). *How fathers care for the next generation: A four-decade study.* Cambridge: Harvard University Press.

St. Claire, M. (1996). *Object relations and self psychology: An introduction* (2d ed.). Pacific Grove, Calif.: Brooks/Cole.

Tillich, P. (1952). *The courage to be.* New Haven: Yale University Press.

Vaillant, G. E. (1977). *Adaptation to life.* Boston: Little, Brown.

Watson, J. B. *Psychological care of infant and child.* New York: W. W. Norton.

Weinfield, N. S., L. A. Sroufe, B. Egeland, and E. A. Carlson. (1999). The nature of individual difference in infant-caregiver attachment. In J. Cassidy and P. R. Shaver (eds.), *Handbook of attachment: theory, research, and clinical applications* (pp. 68–88). New York: Guilford.

Winnicott, D. W. (1965). *The maturational process and the facilitating environment.* New York: International Universities Press.

Wolf, E. S. (1988). *Treating the self: Elements of clinical self-psychology.* New York: Guilford.

Wright, R. (1966). *Black boy: A record of childhood and youth.* New York: Harper and Row.

Wrightsman, L. S. (1994). *Adult personality development. Vol. 1: Theories and concepts.* Thousand Oaks, Calif.: Sage.

Name Index

Subject Index